HELL'S GUEST

To: John —
This book will help
you overcome any
Challenge —
May Many blessings
Come to you, and
yours —
Col. Glenn Frazier
12-3-2012

WWW.COLONELFRAZIER.COM

USAFIRST2008@YAHOO.COM

HELL'S
GUEST

Col. Glenn D. Frazier

Generation Culture Transformation
Specializing in publishing for generation culture change

eGenCo. LLC
824 Tallow Hill Road
Chambersburg, PA- 17202, USA
Phone: 717-461-3436
email: info@egenco.com
Website: www.egenco.com
        www.goingebook.com

facebook.com/egenbooks
twitter.com/vishaljets
youtube.com/egenpub
egenco.com/blog

Hardcover ISBN 978-1-936554-14-0
Paperback ISBN 978-1-936554-16-4
(Formerly self-published 978-0-9717039-5-7)
eBook ISBN 978-1-936554-15-7

First Printing: 2007

Cover design and page layout by Kevin Lepp, www.kmlstudio.com

For Worldwide Distribution, Printed in the U.S.A.
11 12 13 14 15 16 / 15 14 13 12

DEDICATION

This book is dedicated to all the men and women who fought and died in the Philippine Islands during World War II and in the defense of Bataan and Corregidor; and to all those who worked so hard at the time of this War, be it at home or on the battlefields, to save the world from bondage to two world powers that wanted to take away our right to be free and our right to live as God intended us to live—each one determining his or her own destiny.

To the men and women who have proudly worn the uniform in honorable service to our country since the formation of the Republic.

To my dear friend and working partner on Bataan—Gerald Block, who later died a hero on the Hell Ship Arisan Maru. His personal bravery during the fighting was an inspiration to me and to many other American and Filipino scouts and soldiers.

To the families who never knew what happened to their loved ones.

To the men and women who never saw our American flag fly again after the Japanese raised the Rising Sun flag over our dead. Let us never forget the cost of freedom paid with their blood and not shed in vain. Let their sacrifice be a shining light for future generations, proclaiming to the world that freedom must be preserved at all costs.

To my family who suffered long and sorely, waiting to know if I were still alive.

To my cherished friend, Dr. James Strickhausen, who has done so much to support my effort in making this book a reflection of my experiences during a long and difficult time in my life. I give him my special thanks.

Also to my dear wife Elizabeth Terri Frazier, who has spent countless valuable hours preparing *Hell's Guest* for publication, and for her sympathetic understanding about the importance of this time in our history (of which so many people tend to want to change the facts). Her trust in God has helped me understand that I must forgive the Japanese and also forgive myself for the years I would not face my real problem. Her support has always been there for me.

Glenn D. Frazier

ENDORSEMENTS

Hell's Guest is history at its best. Colonel Glenn Frazier's personal account of service, sacrifice, and survival is a riveting page turner. From combat battles in the Philippines, through the unspeakable horrors of the Bataan Death March, and then imprisoned in Japanese slave labor POW camps, Colonel Frazier beat the odds for more than three years and lived to tell us about it!

Colonel Frazier has shared his engrossing story at my college numerous times as part of our "Living Legends" series. Each time, hundreds of students are held spellbound as the lessons of war and its cost are laid out before them. The spirit of America at war is captured in *Hell's Guest*, which is a story that must be told to all generations. Colonel Frazier and the men who served with him are true American heroes and national treasures. As you read this book, you will be reminded that we must never forget their devotion to our nation.

Mike Strouth
Assistant Professor of History
Mountain Empire Community College
Big Stone Gap, Virginia

As gripping a story about life as a POW in World War II as has ever been written, *Hell's Guest* puts the reader right there into the brutal experiences Glenn Frazier remembers so well.

Bill Tunnell, Executive Director
USS ALABAMA Battleship Memorial Park
Mobile, Alabama

Meeting American heroes who have given their all for our country has been one of my greatest privileges as an educator and history buff. I have had the honor to meet two survivors of the Bataan Death March—Colonel Glenn Frazier being the most recent. I not only count Colonel Frazier as a dear friend but a true American hero deserving of the highest honors we can give to an American serviceman. You will not lay this book down until you reach the final page. Truly this man has been blessed to proclaim what it means to sacrifice for his country and then to show us how to forgive those who sought to bring us harm. Glenn's story will definitely be appreciated by all those who understand the supreme sacrifices made by our military to protect the freedoms we enjoy as Americans. Thank you, Colonel, for writing this book.

Edwin J. Van Dongen, Jr.
Middle School American History Teacher (retired)
Grandville Public Schools
Grandville, Michigan

Hell's Guest written by Colonel Glenn D. Frazier is one of the finest books I have been privileged to read. The first time I read this book, I started reading at 8:00 am and finished at 4:00 pm that same afternoon. Since then, I have reread the book three additional times. Colonel Frazier has a captivating style of writing in which it is difficult to put the book down. Having always had an interest in WWII, I have read many other books about this War and have found Colonel Frazier's book to be among the very best. *Hell's Guest* describes the Bataan Death March as if you were there, as well as the atrocities of the Japanese prison camps. His unbelievable ability to forgive the Japanese after the War was accomplished only with the help of God. *Hell's Guest* is a must read for everyone.

CDR Richard N. Howell, Professor
Lansing Community College
Lansing, Michigan

We invited Colonel Frazier to Omaha to speak to several organizations, one of which was a group of high school students seated in a packed auditorium. After hearing the Colonel's story of survival and eventual forgiveness of his captors, a Japanese-American student tearfully apologized for his ancestors. Immediately, Colonel Frazier wrapped his arms around the student and expressed his love for him. Colonel Frazier is a national treasure—it is an honor and privilege to know him.

Bill and Evonne Williams
Patriotic Productions
Omaha, Nebraska

Hell's Guest is a stirring account of a man's courage and determination to survive the terrors of war and the inhumane and unmerciful Bataan Death March. Colonel Glenn Frazier was able to forgive his enemies, and as a result, he is living in true freedom and peace. The people of the world need to read this book and understand how he attained victory. With honor and respect, I salute you, Sir!

Carter Phillips, Evangelist
Henderson, Kentucky

The story of the Bataan Death March and imprisonment as a POW during World War II has never been told better. Colonel Glenn Frazier shares his dreadful experiences most poignantly. Colonel Frazier's story of survival makes him a hero—his story of forgiveness makes him a legend!

Timothy L. Frost
Staff Sergeant (retired)
United States Army

Glenn Frazier is truly a dynamic, charismatic, and compassionate man, and I am honored to say, a personal friend of mine. Over the years, I've spent many hours listening to the experiences that led up to his capture, the Bataan Death March, his imprisonment, and his eventual freedom. Glenn's book, *Hell's Guest*, gives us an intimate glimpse into the physical, emotional, and spiritual battles that he faced. I know God will use this book to not only inspire and encourage future generations, but also heal and give hope to current soldiers, and their families, who are struggling with physical wounds, emotional scars, and memories of recent wars. I am blessed to know Glenn and his beautiful wife, Terri. I know that God has a plan for their lives, and will continue to use them to make a positive impact in many lives throughout the world.

Valentin Obregon
Air Force (retired)
VFW National Chaplain (2009-2010)
Bay Minette, Alabama

Colonel Glenn Frazier's remarkable saga and undaunted spirit will resonate within the human soul. He literally risked his life for God and Country. Colonel Frazier's life demonstrates that the power of forgiveness is greater than the most incomprehensible atrocity that any human being can face in this life. It drove me to my knees.

Eileen Anderson Lancaster
M.S., Special Education (The Johns Hopkins University)
York County, Pennsylvania

An incredible tale of survival, bravery, heartbreak, redemption, and the transformative power of forgiveness. A must read for history buffs, told as only a soldier can tell it. *Hell's Guest* is an inspiring achievement.

John Crane
Television Writer/Producer
Los Angeles, California

Hell's Guest is an engaging World War II story of an adolescent boy propelled into manhood through the horrific experiences of fighting, enduring the Bataan Death March, and merely existing in a Japanese war prison camp for three and one-half years.

Hell's Guest is a moving narrative that unfolds as told by a friend and will never be forgotten by the reader. The unimaginable horrors of war, torture, starvation, and hard labor suffered as a POW clearly reveal the strength and inexplicable desire of humans to survive and return to those who love them...and this strength gives hope for all. This compelling story of Colonel Glenn Frazier, in which forgiveness plays a vital part, cannot be put down until the last chapter is read and his freedom is regained!

Dr. Sarah Allison
Allison Academy
Miami, Florida

The book *Hell's Guest* is a firsthand account of Colonel Glenn Frazier's life experience that *must* be read by every American! I was not able to put this book down and was compelled to get to the next page. It is filled with adventure, drama, tragedy, and triumph—a real story about a boy from Alabama who is thrust into mortal combat against indescribable evil and cruelty. But the story doesn't end with the surrender of the Japanese army. Colonel Frazier returns home to face an unseen enemy inflicting wounds that no doctors can heal.

John A. Wega, Chaplain
Executive Director
United States Christian Commission Museum
Gettysburg, Pennsylvania

Colonel Glenn Frazier's harrowing and heroic story is a constant reminder that the Second World War wasn't the "good war" of our subsequent mythologizing, but the worst war ever, where young men from the heartland sacrificed their innocence, and often a whole lot more, to create the world we now enjoy. Frazier's experience, told here in this extraordinary book, is at once ironic, courageous, horrifying, and ultimately redeeming, and he tells it as only an honest soldier can—straight from the heart.

Ken Burns, Director
PBS documentary, *The War*

TABLE OF CONTENTS

FOREWORD

On April 9th, 1942, General King surrendered Bataan. As we were ordered to the air strip at Maravelles, my thoughts returned to December 8th, 1941 when the Japanese attacked in large formations, bombing Clark Field, Nichols Field, Cavite Naval Base, and Corregidor, destroying 98 percent of all our P-40's, B-17's, and other planes—just sitting there on the runway. The Air Force officers had not been able to obtain clearance to attack from the air when the Japanese 14th Army, one of the best, landed at Lingayen Bay. Subsequently, the Japanese easily walked ashore after some of their ships had already been anchored for 24 hours.

The Death March started for Gerald and me later that afternoon of April 9th, and we marched all through the night. The next morning, as I looked to my right I saw the Rising Sun flag waving on our flagpole, while Old Glory had been tossed onto the ground and was being trampled by the Japanese. My heart was broken, and I felt numb. It was hard to keep going. I pointed to the flag pole for Gerald to see. By the look on his face, I could tell he was feeling the same—we were devastated that we had had to surrender to the enemy.

When I looked ahead, I noticed a Japanese cameraman taking pictures. The one on the cover of this book shows me (third from the left) and my comrade Gerald Block (towel around his neck) early in the march.

Overnight everything had changed. Our freedom had absolutely disappeared. Little did we know that the Japanese would not honor the Geneva Convention rules regarding the treatment of prisoners of war. Everything was gone. We had no constitution to protect us. Americans and Filipinos were being shot or bayoneted to death for falling down or trying to get to an artesian well for a drink of water. There would be no sleep for six days and seven nights. We had nowhere to turn. Our promised reinforcements had never arrived, and we were at the mercy of our captors. If we lived, it would be a miracle.

About 2:00 a.m. on the 7th night, the 90-mile march ended at San Fernando. I could no longer pick up my feet. I just slid them along. My tongue was starting to swell, and I needed to continuously push it back into my mouth. We were herded into a fenced compound, jammed together, and went to sleep standing up. The next day we were loaded onto trains and moved on to Camp O'Donnell.

After 3 1/2 years suffering as a prisoner of war and enduring the endless horrors of slave labor camps, I was a shell of a man amongst very humble men. At the same time, my hatred for the Japanese had grown into an all-consuming force. Someday, I would get even with them.

For the next 40 years, this anger and bitterness festered and ravaged my mind and body. It affected my thinking and reasoning in all areas of my life. For endless nights, I suffered from haunting nightmares. I was always exhausted and could barely digest my food. I couldn't escape the bondage. And I remained a prisoner of my own hatred.

It would be the Word of God that would change my life. Matthew 18:15-35 says,

> [Jesus said], *"If your brother or sister sins, go and point out their fault, just between the two of you. If they listen to you, you have won them over. But if they will not listen, take one or two others along, so that every matter may be established by the testimony of two or three wit-*

*nesses. If they still refuse to listen, tell it to the church;
and if they refuse to listen even to the church, treat them
as you would a pagan or a tax collector. Truly I tell you,
whatever you bind on earth will be bound in heaven,
and whatever you loose on earth will be loosed in heaven.
Again, truly I tell you that if two of you on earth agree
about anything they ask for, it will be done for them by
My Father in heaven. For where two or three gather in
My name, there am I with them." Then Peter came to
Jesus and asked, "Lord, how many times shall I forgive my
brother or sister who sins against me? Up to seven times?"
Jesus answered, "I tell you, not seven times, but seventy-
seven times. Therefore, the kingdom of heaven is like a
king who wanted to settle accounts with his servants.
As he began the settlement, a man who owed him ten
thousand bags of gold was brought to him. Since he was
not able to pay, the master ordered that he and his wife
and his children and all that he had be sold to repay the
debt. At this the servant fell on his knees before him. 'Be
patient with me,' he begged, 'and I will pay back everything.' The servant's master took pity on him, canceled
the debt and let him go. But when that servant went
out, he found one of his fellow servants who owed him
a hundred silver coins. He grabbed him and began to
choke him. 'Pay back what you owe me!' he demanded.
His fellow servant fell to his knees and begged him, 'Be
patient with me, and I will pay it back.' But he refused.
Instead, he went off and had the man thrown into prison
until he could pay the debt. When the other servants saw
what had happened, they were outraged and went and
told their master everything that had happened. Then
the master called the servant in. 'You wicked servant,' he
said, 'I canceled all that debt of yours because you begged
me to. Shouldn't you have had mercy on your fellow
servant just as I had on you?' In anger his master handed*

*him over to the jailers to be tortured, until he should pay
back all he owed. This is how My heavenly Father will
treat each of you unless you forgive your brother or sister
from your heart"* (NIV).

I realized that the Japanese did not even know I existed, and
here I was killing myself with my hatred for them. I asked God for
help. And in time, He changed me. It was a process; I had to take
one day at a time, and deal with one thought at a time. And I had
to pray—all the time. In fact, it would take me about five years to
divest myself of all the hate that had been destroying me. Finally, I
was free—really *free.* And I found that I could love—I could receive
love and give love that for years I had never thought possible.

Colonel Glenn Frazier

1

THE BOY I WAS

No one was in a hurry.

It was the 1930s in southern Alabama where cotton and corn-fields were the backdrop of my childhood stage. I was growing up just like everyone else—wrapped in a simple and predictable way of life. Folks were the same, weather was the same, the calendar was the same. It was such an uncomplicated time that I could never have imagined that in just a few short years the entire world would be engulfed in war and that I would be caught in the middle of it. Where I lived in Lowndes County, events in Europe and Asia, as menacing as they were, seemed light-years away. I would soon discover that they were not so far away after all.

The impact that the Second World War would have on the rest of my life was at that time unthinkable to me, even if I had been forewarned of the details of my own participation: the Japanese attack on the Philippines, the desperate fight for Bataan, the Death March north from the peninsula, and the terrible years, struggling literally every moment for survival as a Japanese prisoner of war. There was nothing in my present mundane experience to measure such things by.

My hometown, Fort Deposit, population 1500, was like many other small towns in the Black Belt of lower central Alabama. And

1

like so many others in the Deep South, we did not have electricity or even running water. Elementary sanitation was relegated to the outhouses that stood at the far limit of every backyard. There was no TV, and even radio programs were often garbled and distorted by static. The icebox was the only way to keep food cool, unless you put the food in a bucket and lowered it into the water at the bottom of the well. Clothes and linens were washed by hand and hung on a line to dry.

We were in the midst of the Great Depression, but my family was better off than most. My father owned a grocery store, and though he was tough on us boys (there were four of us, as well as two sisters), he was a generous man who seldom turned anyone away from his counter because they couldn't pay. I remember that after he died in the 1950s, previous customers still came by to pay off debts they had incurred years before. Dad also owned a mill that ground the best cornmeal in the county.

My mother was what you might call a pillar of the Methodist Church. Friends would visit on Sunday after services were over; and it was the custom that if you invited someone to visit on Sunday, they were also expected to come for dinner. There was always lots of food and fellowship, and on warm days everyone would sit on the front porch to enjoy the faintest of breezes *and* to talk. There was always talk about the wars—they talked about the War between the States—and they talked about the Great War. There was talk about who had gone to serve, talk about the unusual *and* the usual things that had happened to them, and of course, talk about whose family had given the greatest sacrifice. In the meantime, our secluded world seemed to have changed little since those wars had taken place, even those battles that had occurred some 70 years prior. Nevertheless, change, big change, was on the way.

When the Depression began to wane and the economy started to improve, major highways were paved and automobile companies launched the production of fast cars that could take advantage of them. Until that point, you were making darned good time to do 30 or 35 miles per hour on the old, dirt roads. Then came a Ford with a V-8 engine. Man, what a car. It took off lickety split, and could do 70 to 80 miles per hour. My dad bought a shiny, black sedan.

Although he had never been out of the state of Alabama, Dad had a hankering to go to Texas to see an uncle who had moved there by covered wagon, along with his family and few belongings. In 1936, Dad was able to make that trip—and a lot faster than he had ever thought possible—in an automobile.

By 1939, our world was changing fast. Country homes were hooking up to the new electric lines, and by 1940, most homes had electric refrigerators, inside bathrooms, and running water as well. When someone got a washing machine, it was the talk of the town. It was a new era. Life was good, and no one was complaining. Just over the horizon, though, there were storm clouds gathering and a heap-a-trouble coming.

Halfway around the world, and far away from our little corner of the earth, Hitler had overrun Poland, and England and France were under attack. Prime Minister Churchill was doing everything he could to involve America in the war, yet President Roosevelt, who was very conscious of the strong isolationist sentiment in Congress, would promise only material support and supplies, without the troops. In the meantime, patriotic support surged, and every young American male was soon talking about joining one of the military branches just in case we did get in the fight.

As the end of 1940 approached, I was looking forward to graduating from Fort Deposit High School the following May. I was a tall, physically strong young man in the senior class, a forward on the basketball team, and a tackle in football. I was fit, able, and always fixin' to take on any challenge. Nothing seemed too hard for me. I was full of energy and life, and developing a real wanderlust. I thought constantly about the places where I wanted to go, the sights I wanted to see, and the things I wanted to do that I had never done before. In the meantime, I held down different afternoon and weekend jobs. For a while, I worked as a Greyhound bus agent in our town, and also pumped gas for a penny a gallon. In fact, I had built up such a good business, that I was making more money than the average man living in our town who had a family to support. With my savings, I bought my dream-come-true—a 1938 Harley-Davidson motorcycle. Now I had the means to hit the road and high-tail it out of there. And in my mind, the possibilities were endless.

Right away, I began to take road trips to other small towns up to 50 miles away. I thought I was king of the highway and took advantage of my new status by offering girls a ride as often as possible. Fast runs and quick stops meant that they would have to hold on tight. Being the ornery daredevil that I was, I also would stand on the seat while driving as fast as 60 mile an hour. And even one time, at the state fair, on a dare, I drove my Harley inside a cylinder where I rode round and round up the inside wall until I reached the top lip. The centrifugal force kept the wheels of the bike pressed firmly to the side and prevented me and the bike from falling to the bottom. Somehow I managed—I'll never know quite how—to do this trick riding without killing myself.

For some people, there are certain events that, against all expectation, change one's life. So it was with me. It was near the end of the school year when I asked my best and only female friend to go with me to the senior prom. Jamie (not her real name) was a beautiful brunette and sixteen years old. She and I had shared a unique friendship and almost all our secrets since we had met in the first grade. Recently, though, she had been dating a boy from another town. I wasn't quite sure how close they were, but I was certainly glad when I discovered that he could not come to the prom, and she could go with me instead. For obvious reasons, it wouldn't have been reasonable to escort her on my bike on such a formal occasion, so I asked my dad if I could use his car for this important night.

I took more than my usual amount of time getting all gussied up and was anxiously looking forward to spending a special night with a special girl. When the time came to leave, I asked my Dad for the car keys. As he handed them to me, he said, "You'll have to put some gas in the car." I didn't think too much about it, but when I sat down behind the wheel, I noticed that the gauge was on empty. I ran back in the house and let my dad know that there was not even a little gas in the car, and he responded, "Yeah, well, Dowling [my family and friends called me by my middle name], you'll have to buy your own gas for tonight. You certainly always have enough money to keep that dang bike of yours on the road."

But I didn't have enough money, which meant I had no way to take Jamie to the prom. It was just too embarrassing to go to Jamie's house this late and tell her that I could not be her date for the night, nor could I take her out after the prom was over. So…I just didn't go at all. I felt like a heel. And to deal with my grief, I just got on my bike and rode up and down the road, agonizing about the next time I would have to face Jamie and my classmates.

Somehow, Jamie forgave me. Later, when she told me that she would be going to her boyfriend's home on the Fourth of July holiday to meet his parents, I realized how much she truly meant to me, and I was near overcome with jealousy. Afraid that she might get engaged to him, I asked her to go out to a movie with me the night before she was to leave. We started talking, and I decided to find out just how serious their attraction was towards each other.

I was in no mood for a darn movie as thoughts raced through my mind that Jamie was about to leave me and marry another man. So instead, with her on the back of my bike, I drove to a local lovers' lane where we had gone many times before to talk. This time, I kissed her right on the lips, and it was like bells and whistles going off. I reckon' I could have flew to the moon when I discovered that the same feeling came over her. We were locked arm in arm, kissing and crying like two little kids.

For the first time in our lives we knew that our relationship was more than just a friendship. We were deeply in love and could not turn each other loose. And for four hours or so, tears flossed down our faces, words of love were spoken over and over, and promises were made that we would never part. I was totally and completely head over heels and was letting it all out.

Eventually, we came up for a breath of air, and Jamie declared that her trip the next day would be only as a "friendship" trip and that she would tell this other boy that she could not marry him. Even so, I was having none of it. I told her that if she went on this trip, I for darned-sure would not be around when she returned.

It was getting late and still we continued to sit there holding and kissing each other. I finally dragged myself to look at my watch and noticed that it was 3:00 a.m. I did not want this night to end, nor did I want to take her home. But I had to. As we pulled up to her house, we saw that the lights were still on and her mother was waiting on the front porch, looking as though she was fixin' to whoop my butt. As Jamie got off the bike, she whispered to me, "Don't worry. I'm not going."

When I walked her up to the porch, her mother asked, "Where in the tarnation have you two been?" Jamie turned to her mother and said, "I'm not going tomorrow." "Oh yes, you are," her mother shot back. "I ain't havin' you make a promise to someone and then go breakin' that promise without good cause." Her mother then turned to me. "Dowling, I think you had better leave right now. She *is* going on this trip, and whatever she has told you don't mean nothin'."

That night, I was afraid if I went to bed, I would oversleep the next morning and miss going to the train station at 7 a.m. I wanted to see if Jamie would actually go through with it and get on that train. Sure enough, at 7 o'clock, her mother drove up to the station, and I could feel my heart drop when I saw *my* Jamie climb on board. I had never experienced such grief, and I thought my heart would explode. As the train clanked to a start and the engineer blew the whistle, it was like my world had come crashing down, and I couldn't hold back the tears.

By the time it took me to walk to my bike, my tears had already turned to anger. I reminded myself that I had told her I would not be around when she returned, and dawg gonnit, I had meant it! I jumped on my bike and rode as fast as I could back home. I was fit to be tied and so totally consumed by a rage within that I was determined to do something drastic. I ran into the house, hurriedly changed my clothes, and grabbed a set of underclothes. I didn't see any reason to take my hat along, so I stopped for just a second to toss it onto the hall hat rack. I was not certain where I was goin', but sure-as-shootin', I was leavin'. I remember someone saying something to me, but I didn't stop to answer. I jumped back on my bike and stormed off down the road. And the further I rode, the angrier I got. Before I knew what I wanted to do or where I wanted to go, I was in Montgomery, 30 miles north.

I had started out with a full tank of gas, so I continued riding around for a spell, trying to keep my mind occupied with other thoughts. At one point, I wondered if any of my friends would be at the naval recruiting office that day. There had been talk that many boys, instead of looking for a job, were getting their folks to sign for them to go into the service. I glanced inside the recruiting office, but didn't recognize any boys from my hometown. So, I decided to go over to a juke joint where my friends and I regularly hung out when we went to Montgomery.

The owner of this particular joint had once told us to never come back alone because the local boys had been itchin' to pick a fight with us. If we wanted to go in, we had to go, in a group of four or more, and usually after dark. But this time, I plumb didn't care who or what was waiting for me, and I went on in, walked over by the dance floor, and ordered a Coke.

I had noticed a few guys and gals there, but was minding my own business, anguishing over thoughts about the situation between Jamie and me. All of a sudden, the owner walked over towards me and roughly said, "I thought I told you Lowndes County boys not to come in here by yourselves. The guys over there are talking about beating you up. Get the heck out of here, now!"

I sat there staring back at him and calmly replied, "I will leave when I'm darned good-and-ready to leave and...as soon as I drink my Coke." Without a second's hesitation, he snatched the Coke from my hand and shouted, "Get out now, and don't come back by yourself again!"

As I walked to my bike, the anger continued to build up inside. I slowly got on my bike and started toward the road, but all of a sudden, the resentment was more than I could bear. I whipped the bike around, revved the engine, and gunned it for the club's swinging doors. By the time I reached the entrance, I was doing about 45 miles per hour.

The crash bars on the bike took out the right door, sending it into a table and chairs like a missile. I then aimed for the big dance floor in the back and cleared a path through other tables and chairs to get there, sending pieces flying across the room.

As guys and girls scattered, running and screaming, I reached the center of the dance floor. Then I gunned the bike again, did a figure eight, and stopped back in the middle of the floor; then shot the gas some more so that the back wheel made a streak all the way across the floor. I finally headed for the exit but not without demolishing another row of tables and chairs. I was spittin' mad.

On my way out, as I looked over toward the bar, I saw the owner coming out of his office with a shotgun in his hands. But before he could round the corner, I was through the left door, taking it out as well, and sending it into the parking lot. Somehow I had the clarity of mind to realize that if I chose to escape by the road, I might have to stop for cars. So I turned and went around to the back of the building, through the bushes and tall grass, across a ditch, up a bank, and into another street. I was out of sight before he could draw a bead on me.

Down the street, I stopped at a gas station, where for some reason, I told the owner, a man I knew, what I had done.

Shaking his head, he said, "Boy, are you in a heap-a-trouble. That man is mean. He will hunt you down and shoot you like a dog."

As I rode away, I wondered how in the world I would ever get out of this mess now. My first idea was to leave my home for good. My girlfriend was on her way to getting married, and I had left an awful mess in that joint. I was so confused and my mind was so warped that I hadn't even noticed where I was driving. After a while, I calmed down somewhat and glanced over to see the Army-Navy recruiting offices in the shopping strip I was passing by. *Well*, I said to myself, *I think it's time to try the Army.*

As I walked into the recruiting office, a sergeant greeted me and asked what had brought me to the office. I said, "I'm here to join the Army." He then asked me, "How old are you, son?" And the words just came out: "It's my birthday—I'm 21 today." I knew I looked older than I was, and I knew also that my parents would never sign for me to join. I had to choose a birth date, so I picked that day—the third of July. It seemed appropriate—tomorrow's date was the beginning of a new nation and so, the beginning of a new life for me.

Within an hour all the paperwork had been completed. A lieutenant then came out of his office, swore me in, and said, "You're in the Army now. Happy birthday."

They gave me three options when asking me where I wanted to go. Alaska was too cold, and the Panama Canal was just too close to Montgomery. I wanted to get as far away as possible. I figured that the bar owner with his shotgun wouldn't have a chance of finding me if I went all the way to the Philippine Islands. So that's where I chose.

By this time, I wasn't so angry, and had calmed down enough to think of how surprised Jamie would be when she returned to find that I'd gone away. I figured she probably would come back, having turned down the other boy's proposal, and would then declare her undying love for me. Of course, I was pretty sure she would wait for me. And it probably wouldn't matter that much to her if she didn't know exactly where I had gone. And you know, a three-year enlistment wasn't that long of a time to wait, right? Well anyway, it was too late to change things now.

Before I left the recruiting office, the officer had given me a train ticket to Hattiesburg, Mississippi, one meal ticket, and a phone number to call when I arrived to let officials from Camp Shelby know to pick me up. First, though, I had to do something with my motorcycle, so I drove to my cousin Jerome's house and asked him to keep my bike while I was away for a spell. I didn't want him, or anyone, to know where I was going, so I also asked him to drop me off at the bus station. If he had taken me to the train station, he most likely would have suspected that I was going on a longer trip. To avoid any further suspicion, I told him he could ride my bike while I was gone for a month or so.

As I waited for the train to Hattiesburg, the lieutenant from the recruiting office came into the station and handed me a brown envelope. It contained orders for two black recruits to report to Camp Shelby as well. He informed me that this was my first assignment and to make sure that these two guys got off in Hattiesburg and went with me to the camp.

However, at the very next stop, these two guys were already trying to get off the train. All the way to Hattiesburg, I had to keep my eye on them, constantly walking back to their car to make sure they stayed on. And at every stop we made, they tried to get off.

When we finally arrived in Hattiesburg, the next morning, both were sound asleep. They had finally given up.

The three of us got off, and I made the phone call to Camp Shelby. I was surprised to learn that we were not expected until the 5th, and the official reminded me that it was a holiday—the Fourth of July. After making that five-cent phone call, I had twenty cents left and just one meal ticket.

The two black men then asked me to get them something to eat. When I talked to the station restaurant manager and explained our situation, he agreed to feed the other two men, but then said to me, "I reckon' you should have had better sense than to leave Montgomery without any money." I couldn't believe it—he fed them, but not me. There I was, spending the Fourth of July broke and alone, when I was sure that back home, my family was celebrating as usual, with a picnic, all the fixins, and plenty of watermelon.

The camp officials finally showed up later that afternoon. The first thing on my mind was to tell them that I needed something to eat. Well, the mess hall was closed that day, but thankfully, when we got to the camp, they made us all some sandwiches.

My first orders included handing in the papers for the two black men, and then I was escorted to a tent where I was to remain until they processed us through. The tent was one of those semi-permanent jobs with a canvas top and a wooden floor, with three feet of wood siding and wire screening stretched up to the roof. It was large enough to house eight bunk beds. At the edge of the canvas were several ropes that anchored it into the ground. When it rained, we would have to tighten the ropes to keep the rain from collapsing the tent.

Here at Camp Shelby, it didn't take long to meet my first hard-nosed drill sergeant. His name was Jones, but we called him "Bulldog." At 6 a.m. every day, he would blow that cotton-pickin' whistle loud enough to hear five blocks away. Then he would yell,

"All right, you dogfaces, up and at 'em." When he blew that darned whistle, the spit would fly about three yards from his mouth. I never knew another person who could blow a whistle and yell at the same time, like he could. He also had a hankerin' for walkin' alongside the tents, and beatin' on them with a stick.

He rode us hard from morning to night. His yellin' and blowin' that whistle was as bad as the stink on a wet dog. There was no pleasin' the man. Once, I had the courage to ask him, "Why do you yell so much?" His answer: "Frazier! This is the Army, and you isn't seen nothing yet! You dogfaces will have to shape up or ship out!"

Rising in the morning, ready and outside in 15 minutes, was really hard to do, but you darned better not come out with your shirttail hangin' or your shoes undone. The sergeant was specific with his instructions, and everyone knew if you didn't follow them, you'd be placed on KP. *What the heck was KP?* I thought. *It didn't sound so bad.* Well, I found out the hard way. Kitchen Police duty was dawg-gone tough—cleaning up the mess hall, peeling potatoes, scrubbing pots and pans, and doing whatever other dirty work the mess sergeant needed done.

In that part of Mississippi in July, it rained almost every afternoon, sometimes three or four times a day. And the minute the rain started, the sergeant would blow that dang whistle and yell, "All out to loosen the ropes!" It was often miserable. Then the rain would stop, and here he would come again, yellin' for us to tighten the tent ropes. That could happen several times a day, and usually did.

When we were not assigned to KP, the sergeant would place us on other work detail, which was just fine by me. I didn't want to sit around and listen to a bunch of no' count, good-for-nothin' draftees complain all the time. I guess I heard about every story in the book.

Then came the day when we were to be issued our first uniforms. We were ordered to walk past a long counter where four men on the other side were grabbing shirts, pants, GI underwear, shoes, and socks out of boxes, and then tossing them across to us. No particular thought was given to size—you got whatever was thrown at you. Sergeant Bulldog yelled, "Stop bitchin'! Trade with each other if you want somethin' that fits; otherwise, wear what you're given!"

I had never seen such a motley-lookin' bunch as we were when we turned out that evening to march to mess hall. It was plumb disgraceful. Some had shirts that fit like gunnysacks covering extra-long pants that had to be rolled up from the bottom. Other pants were too short and hitched about a foot up their legs. For me, I couldn't get a cap to fit, so they gave me a World War I issue. How in the name of sense were we to look like soldiers for inspection the next day? And when the time came for the captain to pass by the troops, he was flabbergasted. "Sergeant, where did these men get their clothing?"

"GI issue, Sir!"

"Please! Hide them until I can get something done."

It took about four days, but finally, we got to trade in shirts, shoes, and pants for a better fit. Even so, we still looked like rejects from a used clothing store. And we stayed that way until our orders came to ship out. Then, thank goodness, it became a more important matter that we appear presentable-like for the trip to California.

What a great day it was to receive orders to finally escape Camp Shelby. Twenty-five of us were headed to Angel Island in the San Francisco Bay, and with a buck sergeant in charge, we loaded onto Pullman cars, each with a ten-dollar advance pay as a little pocket change.

We all were more than glad to be on our way. Some were going to Hawaii, some to Guam, and a few, like me, to the Philippines. The southern boys from Alabama, North Florida, and Mississippi were especially thrilled with the idea of travelling west. It was exciting to cross the great Mississippi River at Baton Rouge, Louisiana, and then travel on to the big city of Dallas, Texas. Then on to New

Mexico, Colorado, Utah, and Nevada, and on into California—places we had never seen before.

At times, my thoughts would drift back to home, wondering if Jamie had returned. *Was she engaged? Would she be getting married? Did she miss me?* I would also think of my family, and feelings of guilt would surface because as far as I knew, they still had no idea where I was. I had been very careful not to tell a soul that I had joined the Army, and every so often the thought nagged me that someone would find out I had lied about my age and then I would be sent home.

But for today, I was sure thrilled to see the sights. As we traveled west into the Texas Panhandle, I never thought it possible for one to look so far without seeing trees. The land was just...bare. On into the night, we traveled into northern New Mexico and were told that our Pullman cars would be side-railed and we would have to wait for another train to pick us up. When we woke up the next morning, I looked out the window again and still was amazed to discover that I could not see a single tree...all the way to where the mountains jutted out of the horizon. It was like we had landed on the moon or something. I woke up everyone else saying, "Look, fellas, there are no trees in sight." We all stared out the window, and within the next few minutes, we were all standing outside, dumb-founded, gazing in all directions, unable to stop talking about this phenomenon.

About an hour later, a train came and hooked up our cars. We traveled on through Colorado, and were flat-out stunned at the sight of the Rocky Mountains. Our seven-day trip from Camp Shelby to California was one of the most amazing experiences that had ever happened to me and for the other Southern boys as well.

When we arrived at the train station in San Francisco, the sergeant ordered us to remain in the terminal, and not to take even one step outside the building. Well, after about an hour, four of us got a little antsy and decided that nothing could be hurt by walking outside to see just a little piece of San Francisco.

As we stood alongside the building, it wasn't long before four men dressed in red, white, and blue uniforms, with all kinds of brass buttons, came around the corner. We had never seen anyone so dressed up. They seemed to be on a mission, and were headed straight towards us, at a pace. As they approached, we boys being Southern-born and raised, spoke up. "Howdy, boys, how y'all doin'?"

The next thing we knew the four of us hit the wall, each with a busted nose and our eyes swelling shut. Ribs were cracked and bodies were bruised. They still didn't say a word, just laughed and walked on down the sidewalk. As we were pulling ourselves up off the ground and trying to get ourselves together and back into the terminal, the sergeant reappeared. "What in the Sam Hill happened to you?"

Hesitantly, we told our story. Then with somewhat of a grin, the sergeant replied, "Gentlemen, you have just met the United States Marine Corps."

The sergeant had just arranged our transportation by ferry to Angel Island, and we arrived there after dark on July 18th. But I could tell already that it was going to be a much better place than Camp Shelby. There were hundreds of men everywhere, waiting to board a ship to the Far East. Most were recruits, like us, headed out for a hitch of three years. There were men from all parts of the USA, and most were volunteer regular Army like me. In fact, I didn't meet one draftee. Many of the men in our barracks were in the Army Air Corps and were going to Hawaii—to Hickam Field. I continued to meet some of the most interesting people, and there was one guy who I especially will never forget.

Hal's bunk was next to mine. He had joined the Army of his own accord, like the rest of us, and was going to the Philippine Islands, like me. Hal (not his real name) was one of a kind, and bitched about everything. I figured there wasn't a soul on earth who would mind that I *didn't* smoke, but Hal sure did. He threw a fit that they had assigned someone next to him who had no money *and* didn't smoke, which meant that he couldn't bum any cigarettes from me.

If Hal was good at anything, it was bumming. He was the best panhandler I had ever run into. He had no problem walking up to anyone and asking for a cigarette, promising to pay the person back on the next payday. Yet I heard him calculating that with his Army pay, it would take him six months to pay back everyone that he had bummed a smoke from—as if it was a goal he was proud to have reached. He would also do what we called "shoot butts on the ground," gathering enough to roll a smoke, but all the while complaining about not having proper paper to roll his smokes.

It wasn't long before the officers lined us up for inspection, and as they looked us over, they told most of us that we needed to go and get a haircut, which was 25 cents at the camp barbershop. But many of the guys didn't have two nickels to rub together, so the officers requested that we each receive a partial pay of ten dollars. Man, that ten bucks looked like a million.

Well, it was no surprise that the first thing Hal did was go to the PX (post exchange) and get a carton of smokes. I mean, you talk about what is important in a guy's life. He put a couple of cigarettes in his shirt pocket and stuck the rest of them in his Army bag. Later that day, a guy, who Hal had bummed a smoke from, asked Hal for a smoke in return. Hal refused, saying he didn't have a smoke, then immediately turned to me and said, "See, Frazier, that's why I won't carry a pack with me. All these bums would want their smokes paid back!" This guy was unreal.

Another day, he walked up to a guy and begged a smoke. I knew Hal had some of his own cigarettes in his pocket, so I asked him, "How in the name of sense can you keep doin' this?" He replied, "I don't want to forget how to do it. We might not get another pay until we get to the Philippines."

In the meantime, we were required to get that haircut. And by the time we got to the barbershop, there was a line about two blocks long. No surprise, Hal bitched all the way until he got into that chair. Then he proceeded to tell the barber that he had waited in a line a mile long, and while it was sure nice to get to sit down, he wanted his hair cut just the way he wanted his hair cut. By the time he got those few words out of his mouth, the barber snapped the sheet away from Hal's neck and yelled, "Next!"

Hal looked in the mirror, and saw that his head was as smooth as a cue ball. In the very next breath, Hal started complaining that the barber hadn't cut it like he wanted it, and he demanded his quarter back.

"You want to get out, or you want me to put you out!?" It was more of a seriously strong suggestion than a question.

Hal slowly walked out the door, yet all the while complaining about what a rip-off that haircut had been.

There was never a dull moment with this guy. As we walked back to our barracks, we met up with a captain and a lieutenant, and Hal proceeded to snap up both hands and give them a double salute. With a look of half-confusion, half-disgust on his face, the captain asked him, "Why did you use both hands?"

"Well, there were two of you," Hal said.

The officers didn't think that was too funny. They made him stand there, and taught him a lesson about using one hand. He had to go through the exercise at least ten times. A person would think that he might have learned to change his ways. Not Hal. When we walked off, he carelessly remarked, "I know how to salute the right way, Frazier; I did it the other way for the hell of it." He was always doing something to buck the system.

When the officials came around asking if anyone wanted to set up a personal account in the Bank of America before they left the States, Hal declined, saying that eleven dollars a month wasn't even enough to keep him in smokes. Personally, I figured I would save ten dollars a month during a three-year hitch, which would certainly help when I returned. We had already been told that things were very cheap in the Philippine Islands, so why would I need more money there?

While staying on Angel Island was certainly a step up from Camp Shelby, it was still hard getting adjusted to Army life. Hoping for better days ahead, I continued to watch the bulletin board each day to see if my shipping orders had been posted, and after eleven days, my name came up. I had been assigned to the USS Cleveland, originally a passenger liner that had been converted into a troop ship.

It was a breathtaking sight to sail under the Golden Gate Bridge that afternoon. As I looked back at the mountains fading out of sight, I finally choked up inside. Standing on the fantail, I thought of home. I thought of Jamie. I thought about that angry club owner, wondering if he was still trying to find me. And…I thought about my mother. She didn't know where I was. No one did. It was 1941, I was 16, a naïve boy barely out of school, alone, and on my way around the world. I would be serving in a strange land and living among people I knew nothing about. For better or for worse, I was leaving my home behind. Ready, I thought, for whatever lay ahead.

2

THE BEGINNING...
AND END OF PARADISE

Crossing the Pacific Ocean aboard the President Cleveland proved to be quite an adventure. Some mornings the water would be as slick as glass, with not so much as a wrinkle of a wave. Other days were different. Before we arrived in Guam, we would sail through the meanest of storms in which the waves rose so high over the sides of the ship that they broke over the top of us. Almost everyone on board got more than a little sick.

In a way, the rough seas were easier to handle than the calm. It was especially during the quiet times that I spent many hours thinking about what had happened just before I left the States. Sometimes I was full of regret. Sometimes I experienced remorse. Sometimes I wished that I were back home. Homesickness on top of seasickness was almost unbearable.

Finally, we approached the Philippines and mercifully, my mind was again occupied by other sights and sounds. As we sailed through the Manila Straits, we could see dense jungle off to both sides of the ship. Looking out over Manila itself, we could make out a green countryside with one high-rise building towering above the trees. Soon we could also see the outline of the Pasic River that ran through the city. Once again, I began to look forward to exploring this new country and getting to know its people and their ways. Meeting new people was always something I had enjoyed.

August 7th was a scorching hot day when we docked at the pier in Manila. As the sun beat down hard on us from a cloudless, hazy sky, we American soldiers were greeted by a band playing and a group of Filipinos dancing in the streets. We had been at sea for what seemed a very long time, and we could hardly wait to join them.

It took about an hour to get off the ship and into the parking lot. When we disembarked, there was a pleasant sort of chaos all around us as Army guys yelled, "Thirty-first Infantry!" in addition to the names and numbers of different units. There were seven of us going to the air wing at Nichols Field, and we were told that an Army or Air Corps unit would be by shortly to pick us up. Hal and I said goodbye for now, and made plans to meet at a later date.

Trucks continued to pull up and load all kinds of soldiers. In the meantime, not one person yelled out the name of our unit or showed up for those of us assigned to Nichols Field. Soon the lot was empty, and there we stood, seven men in the middle of a vacant parking lot, having no idea where to go or what to do. We felt somewhat lost and abandoned, but displayed the usual male bravado as we joked and waited…and waited.

At one point, a jeep came by, and we were asked where we were supposed to go, and then it left again. Then we waited for another hour. Finally, trucks arrived, and thankfully, they were there to pick us up. We found out that the air wing to which we had been assigned was presently out on maneuvers, and we were to be taken to the 75th Ordinance Company for housing until our wing came back.

To our pleasant surprise, the ordinance location was just a mile from the docks. The 75th Ordinance Company was an old Army unit that had been set up along with others after the Spanish lost control of the Philippine Islands at the turn of the century. The company's job was to supply ammunition and services to the Philippine Department of the Army, and included a machine shop to rebuild ordinance equipment. The machine shop itself was located in Fort Santiago, within the Walled City of old Manila.

The barracks were apparently the same as the Spanish Army had used and included a mess hall, barbershop, orderly room, and a PX, with the sleeping quarters upstairs. The PX was owned by the 75th Ordinance, and its profits went for programs, parties, or functions for the 135 men in the company. The men of the 75th consisted mostly of soldiers who had ten or more years in the service, and it was almost impossible for anyone else to get into that unit. Many of them were married to Filipino women and had children, and many of them had never been back to America since they had arrived for their first hitch. Ultimately, they planned to retire and remain in the islands for the rest of their lives.

Colonel George Hurst, a fine soldier, was the 75th's commander; and First Sergeant Warren was an easygoing type person who got along with everyone. When stationed in Manila, the men of the 75th would work only half days and were able to go anywhere on the island when off duty. But when assigned on field trips to Bataan, they worked from sunup to sundown. By the time I got there, the Department of Engineers was building warehouses on Bataan, and the 75th was filling them with ordinance. It was common knowledge that if war did come, that's where we would go—Bataan.

When we arrived at the company barracks, our welcoming party consisted of Master Sergeant Warren and two drunk American soldiers. After listening to a few basic rules, it didn't take long for us to realize that this location was a paradise on earth—with great access to downtown. Furthermore, we were not expected to do any work, because the company had hired Filipinos as KP. Imagine that, no KP! We would be required to fall out with the company first thing each day, but right after morning roll call, we would be dismissed. Life was going to be great!

Our first pass came that weekend. We had heard many stories about Manila—its Benny Boys, girls, and cab drivers. We were given one specific warning—not to travel alone when visiting town because the natives were pretty savvy when it came to new recruits and would be sure to take advantage of us. So, I decided to heed the advice and find some suitably husky companions for my first venture into town. My choices were the farm boy from Minnesota and the guy from South Dakota. We figured a combination of the three of us would be plenty enough to keep each other safe. We had almost no money, but that didn't matter. True to what we had been told, things were good and cheap.

As we began walking towards town, we noticed that four cabs promptly began to follow us, so we hopped in the first one behind us. And wham! No sooner had the doors slammed shut than the driver took off on the wrong side of the street towards the bridge leading into town, the horn blaring every inch of the way. *What in the world did we just do?* It was like stepping into a rocket. It seemed as though every cab in town was trying to get over that bridge side by side. What a nightmare of a ride! The driver missed a light pole by about a quarter of an inch, and we had to hold on for dear life during the entire ride.

Somehow we all managed to make it to the Manila side without losing an arm or a leg. I had experienced some pretty wild rides in my day, but this one beat all. In fact, it was so truly terrifying that I wished I had been back in Alabama sitting on my old mule and enjoying a smooth, unhurried gait. As soon we got out of the cab, my two friends fervently thanked God the ride was over, and that we had survived. We all agreed that walking back to the barracks, in lieu of riding again, was our best bet.

Exploring the streets of Manila, we were surrounded by the sights and exotic smells of all types of unusual foods, while peddlers crowded around us trying to sell us their various goods. Little kids, pimping for their "mothers" or "sisters," would beg us to go to their house in return for ten pesos, then reduce the price to five pesos when we didn't take their first offer. At one point, we passed by two well-known massage parlors that most servicemen frequented because they could get about anything they wanted there. From the grunts, groans, and laughs we could hear coming from behind the thin walls, I believed it. We skipped that entertainment.

We then decided to go to a place called the Poodle Dog Club. Just as we stepped through the door, however, there was a charge of people headed toward us, and leaving in a hurry. Chairs were flying through the air, and tables were falling in pieces to the floor. A big fight was in progress, with soldiers and sailors at it hard and heavy. Whistles were blowing, and soon the MPs (military police) and SPs (security police) were all over the place. Nearly everyone scrammed out one of the three doors leading to the streets. In the end, the police didn't take anyone in…this time; they simply told the bartender they would stay close by in case the culprits came back. We found out that about every 30 minutes a good fight would break out—just part of the atmosphere at the Poodle Dog Club.

We ambled on to the Southeastern Hotel and decided to visit a bar on the top floor, famous for a drink called the Gallywacker, made with several shots of whisky, rum, rice wine, and God knows what else. As we walked in, we noticed parallel yellow lines about two feet apart leading from the bar to the cashier. If you could drink two Gallywackers, it was said, and walk to the cashier without stepping on the yellow lines, the two drinks were free.

While we were there, one of the guys from Texas declared that he could drink the two Gallywackers and make it all the way. So, while all the rest of us drank San Miguel beer, Tex finished his second Gallywacker and sat there bragging about how he wasn't drunk at all, and he was dawg-gone sure he could walk to those "yeller" lines without so much as a bobble. All eyes were on him as he proceeded to get up from his chair, and then…fell flat on his face—hard.

It took a couple of us to help him to his feet, and we had to continue to hold him up as he insisted that we guide him to the lines again. When we finally turned him loose, he stumbled backwards into the bar. The bartender then felt it necessary to come over to explain to Tex that you had to go forward, not backwards, to win the two drinks. It took us about 20 minutes to get him out of that bar, down the elevator, and into the street.

Although we had sworn we wouldn't ever take another taxi ride, we ended up getting into another cab that very same day. Once again, we had to hang on for dear life, and we counted our blessings when we arrived at the front door of our compound.

The funny thing was, Tex was totally sober up top; it was his legs that wouldn't function. So, we took him up to the second floor and tossed him on to his bunk where he slept until the next day.

My pay was 21 dollars a month, less the ten dollars I deposited in the Bank of America. This left me with 11 dollars a month of spending money. Since the rate of exchange was two pesos to the dollar, I had 22 pesos a month to spend. Beer was ten centavos—or five cents American money—at our PX, so obviously, I, along with most others, drank San Miguel beer. As I mentioned, the company had hired a group of Filipinos to do all KP. For six pesos a month that the company paid, not one soldier had to wash clothes, cut hair, shine shoes, or clean up the barracks. It was like living at a luxury hotel.

After waiting seven days for our air wing to return, Sergeant Warren called the seven of us down to the dayroom and informed us that he had room in the 75th if any of us wished to transfer in. For most of us, this was a no-brainer. Many of us had not yet attended boot camp training, but we had heard stories and had seen the poor suckers, who came over with us on the USS Cleveland, marching up and down the 31st Infantry parade field sweating and swearing. For darned sure, we had no desire to undergo that kind of training when our air wing came back, so it didn't take long to give Sergeant Warren an answer, and he didn't have to twist any arms to force us to sign up.

He also told us we could go to the Ordinance Training School instead of boot camp, and those of us with grades of 80 or above could become Ordinance Officers in the Philippine Department and assigned to a Philippine Island Army base. If we served three years, we would then be eligible to attend Officers' Candidate School when we returned to the States. This sounded like a good deal. An officer made a lot more money than an enlisted man, and we all seriously considered this option.

At one point, two of my comrades, Gerald and Luke, and I made friends with one of the Filipino bosses at the depot, a guy named Vargas. He liked hanging out with us and soon began inviting us to go with him on weekend trips. He had previously been a guide in the Philippine Islands and so he knew the best places to fish and hunt, and all about everything else there was to do for recreation.

On our next weekend off, we four decided to take one of the personnel carriers, use approved PX funds to pay for the gas, and go on a wild boar hunt. Armed with old 1906 .45 caliber revolvers that were used against the Hucks before World War II, we also got permission to check out M-I carbines for our trip and were anticipating a great hunt. Little did we know that we'd become the hunted.

As we rode along in the carrier, Vargas led us on extremely narrow roads into the heavy jungle in the Bataan area. Every so often, we would be stopped by some Filipino men asking us where we were going. In their language, Vargas would explain what we intended to do for the day, and each time, the Filipino people would graciously tell him in their opinion the best places to hunt wild boar.

As we continued to travel deeper into the jungle, it wasn't long before Vargas spotted a sow with piglets off to our left. As we came to a stop, all four of us casually jumped out of the vehicle to check out the animals. We did not realize it, but the daddy boar of this little family was just across the trail, and he was nothing if not mean. All of a sudden, we could hear that wild boar charging us from behind.

Now, let me tell you, an angry wild boar is not to be trifled with. We all started yelling like girls and running around the personnel carrier shooting our 45s, while this crazy beast was attacking the tires on the truck and chasing us all around. Meanwhile, Vargas was yelling his head off for everyone to calm down. Eventually, all of us made it back to the safety of the truck, scrambling for our lives and climbing over each other to do so. Vargas was upset. There was no way, he said, that he was going to stay in the jungle with us shooting like wild men. Needless to say, it was a mutual decision to end the wild boar hunt pronto and drive north instead to visit some villages. The idea came up to go into the hills and even visit a Negrito tribe.

This option was much more appealing to me. I had heard that the Negrito tribes were some of the earliest humans to settle the Philippines, and that they continued to practice very ancient customs. Walking into one of these tribal communities would be like walking back thousands of years in time.

As we continued our journey up the mountain, we first came to a small village where the kids ran out into the road to see us, excited and waving. Vargas told us that these children had never seen American soldiers before. The children were then followed by many of the adults who also came out to see the strange men in strange clothes. The older folks were gracious as well, wanting to talk to Vargas as well as to the rest of us. Some of the kids were curious enough to come close enough to touch our skin. It was as though we were movie stars, and we got a big kick out of it.

As we drove away, the children ran along behind us, waving and yelling. The folks had given us further direction on how to find the Negrito village, and so we continued on our way up the mountain.

As we negotiated the winding road, monkeys high in the trees, began to scream and continued to do so all along the way, warning other monkeys up ahead that danger was approaching. It was very amusing. It was the first time I had seen monkeys in the wild, and it sounded and looked as if there were hundreds of them.

Eventually we came to a point where we had to get out and walk the rest of the way to the village. Valgras claimed that the Negritos were already aware someone was coming because of the noise the monkeys were making. These animals would someday turn out to be a great alarm system for us as well.

As we followed Vargas along the path, we soon met two men, about four feet high with gray curly hair and dark skin, each carrying a bolo—a long knife, much like a machete. After conversing with Vargas for a few minutes, the one man—the head of the tribe—told us that we were welcome to come to their village. As we walked on, we soon came upon eight grass shacks with a clearing in the center. These nomadic people usually lived in houses made of grass and branches. Five or six kids came out from each shack, while several women and some younger men continued to stare curiously at us. The women wore wrap-around skirts, while the men were covered with only a loin cloth.

They would not come close at first, until the two old men gave their approval and told them to come out and greet us. Then they came forward and made a motion that seemed to be a sign of welcome and told Vargas they thought we were giants. We discovered that only one of them had ever been down the mountain to a village, and not one of them had ever been to a town of any size.

Some people have compared the Negrito tribes to the aborigines of Australia or the pygmies in the jungles of Africa. These people practiced ancient customs, used specific dances for special occasions, and believed in supreme beings who ruled over spirits that inhabited the sky, mountains, valleys, rivers, and other places. We found them to be experts in weaving and plaiting, making baskets, rattan hammocks, and other household containers. We could also see that they intentionally scarred their bodies in order to "decorate" themselves. Obviously, they were masters of life in the rainforest, and I later learned that some from other tribes were employed by the US Army to teach soldiers how to survive in the jungle.

Needless to say, these Negrito people were much friendlier than the irate boar we had met earlier that day. It was an experience that I will never forget.

The next weekend, Vargas invited me to go with him again, this time to a province south of Manila to meet some of his friends and family. After riding the train about 25 miles to a small town, we were met at the station by Vargas' brother and several of his friends. On our way to the brother's house, Vargas told me he wanted me to meet a nice Filipino girl who he described as "not like the ones in Manila." I started to wonder what this trip was really all about.

After we arrived at the house, I was immediately introduced to five girls who all seemed to be close to my age. And when Vargas came to the one girl, he turned to me and said, "This is a very special girl I want you to meet. Her name is Nelda." Nelda was certainly pretty and very nicely dressed. Her hair was long, and she had a beautiful smile. The first words she said to me were, "I've heard a lot of good things about you," and she said them in perfect English.

I thanked her, and she invited me to the dining table for some lemonade. And so started the beginning of an unexpected and peculiar relationship.

The table was covered with fruit and other plants grown nearby. And the main dish was to be a barbecued pig that they were already cooking out in the backyard. The barbecuing technique was rather special. They would trap the pig in a small pen that restricted its movement, and then feed it all it could eat until it was as fat as they wanted it to become. Then they gave it a laxative to clean it out. Next, they would feed the pig rice with a highly seasoned sauce.

The minute the pig stuffed himself with the rice, they would kill it! Then they would run a steel rod into its mouth and all the way through the pig, hang the rod and pig above a fire, and roast the entire body. And I must say, the meat was wonderful.

After we ate that day, Nelda and I walked to a park a few blocks away. I could tell she really liked me—more than any of the girls I had met in Manila. After spending some time at the park, Nelda then wanted me to go right away to her house and meet her family. I agreed, but I wasn't about to make any kind of commitment. And then, there was this nagging thought in the back of my mind. Memories of home. *Did my girl Jamie also do this—meet "the family" but not make a commitment?*

I had just met this girl, and I was already meeting her family. This was pretty heady stuff. In my mind, things were moving fast. Yet at the same time, it was kind of nice to have a pretty girl be so interested and pay attention to me in this way.

As we walked into the house, she introduced me to her father and said, "Dad, this is my new friend—Glenn—a US Army private from the 75th Ordinance. He is visiting here today with Vargas. This is the soldier he talked to you about." I had no idea what Vargas had said or what all these people had in mind for me.

Her father thanked me for coming and asked that I have a seat. Then her mother came into the room, and she also gave me a great welcome. Then came her three brothers and two sisters! For sure, they were all fine-looking people, well-mannered, and extremely kind. They asked where I was from in America and wanted to know about my family. After we talked for a while and had a pleasant visit, Nelda and I started to walk back to the other house. On our way, Nelda asked if we could stop at the park again, saying she wanted to show me something.

At the far end of the park was a large wire cage, inside of which were several monkeys. As we stood looking at these creatures, she pointed out the mother monkey and the father. She explained that they were married, and all the other monkeys were their children. Then she looked up at me and asked if I wanted to get married someday. My answer was, "Sure." She said she liked Americans and could be very happy if she were married to one.

This was strange and a little uncomfortable. I knew Nelda liked me, but I could not stop thinking about Jamie. I had told myself that I would not let myself get involved with anyone until I knew what my Jamie had done. But even so, I pulled Nelda close to me for a small kiss. She held me tight and said that mine was the sweetest kiss she had ever had. She was simply adorable, and I knew right then we had better get back to her house. Our original plans had been to stay there Saturday night, but when we reached the house, Vargas said we had to go back to our base. At that point it was fine with me. The temptation was becoming quite a challenge.

The following Wednesday afternoon Sergeant Warren called me to the dayroom, and when I walked into the room, I was surprised to see Nelda standing there. She said she had come to Manila specifically to see me. As pretty as she was, I was proud to take her to the PX and show her off to the guys in the company. She got along well with other people and was not a standoffish kind of person. I really liked that about her.

It wasn't long after I met Nelda, I found out that a work detail to Bataan would be posted on the schedule. We were not sure that any of us new guys would be sent, but the older guys were determined that us young'uns would be going as well and that they would work the hell out of us. That Saturday, an order was posted on the dayroom board, listing everyone who was to leave early on Monday. And sure enough, all seven of us were on it. Tex, though, was determined that he wasn't going. His plan was to get so hammered he could stay in Manila, and sure-as-shootin', at the time of the Monday morning 6 a.m. wake-up call, Tex was so drunk he had to be carried to the truck. Sergeant Warren told us to load him into the back of one of the trucks and throw his foot-locker in with him.

It was a long haul—130 miles—from Manila to our post in Bataan. The roads were part gravel and very rough and dusty. It was a hard trip. I was one of several drivers who drove a big Corbit truck with tandem back wheels. It was the biggest truck I had ever driven. Once there, we camped out under large jungle trees in pup tents, two persons to a tent—not quite the same type of luxury accommodation that we were used to in Manila. Our mess hall, as we called it, was a wooden-floored tent with a canvas top, with no doors or windows; and our supply warehouses were close by.

While at Bataan, our job was to unload barges of ammo, stack them into our trucks, and deliver them to the 70 warehouses in the jungle that the engineers had built for us and 70 more for the quartermasters. As we started to unload, I asked the sergeant-in-charge why the quartermaster corps wasn't putting supplies into their own warehouses at Fort William McKinley. He informed me that the colonel had ordered that the ammo go directly into our field warehouses so we would not have to handle them a second time.

The rains came, and we kept working, and loading 500-pound bombs. Sometimes the loads were so heavy that we had to pull a truck uphill with a bulldozer...but nothing stopped us. We had a great many tons to load, and we worked hard and fast. We all knew the quicker we got it done, the quicker we could go back to the easy life in Manila.

When we eventually returned to Manila, my thoughts would often drift back to home and to my folks. As far as I knew, they still had no idea that I was in the Philippine Islands—10,000 miles away from Lowndes County. I finally decided it was time to write and sent a letter to my parents on November 15, 1941. It was a short handwritten note, explaining that I had joined the Army and was safe and sound in Manila of the Philippine Islands.

As November was coming to an end, several of us decided to start going more often to the bars during our trips to downtown Manila. One place in particular—the Marouka Bar happened to be a place where Japanese would also come to drink, and most of the time there would be a few Japanese sailors hanging around in there. In this particular establishment, there was a jukebox with keys that you could push down for a selection and then flip back up and change the song before the first record would play. At times, one of the American soldiers would put a dime in to play a song. And then as soon as he would walk away and return to his table, the Japs would come up and change the song to some Japanese record they preferred.

One night there were about 20 to 30 Japanese sailors in the club. A few of us decided to return to our company to tell the others about the many Japs who were there and who were up to their same ole irritating tricks. Before we returned to the bar, we scraped up all the money we could so that everyone would have enough for a couple of beers. Then we spread ourselves out so that we entered the club in groups of four or five at a time. Finally, when our company was all inside, a couple of us went over to the jukebox and selected a few records, and sure enough, them Japs came and pushed up our keys and chose to play a different song—a Jap song. The minute the song started, we all got up and grabbed the nearest Jap to us. We broke up all the tables, chairs, mirrors, *and* the bar. We beat the bartender and laid out all the Japs on the floor. If one started to get up, he'd be hit again in the head with a beer bottle.

It wasn't long before we heard the MPs and SPs coming in the front and starting up the stairs. We high-tailed it out the back, down onto the roof, then to the street, and faded away into the dark. No one was caught. When we were notified that the MPs would be around with the bartender to identify the ones who beat him, the guilty parties were promptly sent to Bataan before any charges could be made. The last we heard, the Japs were insisting that the Army pay for all the damages.

Soon after, Sergeant Warren talked the commanding officer into having a party at the compound. It had been some time before we arrived that the company had had their last beer party, and the sergeant thought it would be a good idea for us to have one before we had to go back to Bataan. The KP boys were to serve beer and handle a big dinner for us, and we could invite one person to the party if we wished.

I attended alone, and as I was eating, a guy who I had previously had some words with started flipping olives from a knife across the table at me. I told him to stop, but he chose not to listen. So, I reached over the table and dragged him over onto my side, and we started to fight.

Everyone was half drunk. One group circled around me with a few holding me, while another group gathered and held him. He was able to break loose, however. In a flash, he grabbed up a butcher knife and then came charging at me, plunging it into my groin about four inches deep. The knife cut a main artery, and blood was spouting all over the place. In the midst of all the commotion and noise, the next thing I knew, I was laid in the back of a truck while someone held the artery closed all the way to Fort William McKinley Hospital. Had that guy not known to do this, it would have been certain death.

I sent word to Vargas about the knifing, who then relayed the message to Nelda. The next day she came to the hospital to see me and was hysterically crying as though I wouldn't make it. In an attempt to calm her down, I asked that she be permitted to stay and take care of me. When that request was denied, she got real upset, yet there was nothing to be done. Fortunately, within a week, I was out and back at the company compound.

In the meantime, I had enrolled in the ordinance school and program, and between going to school and the work on Bataan, I was staying busy. In the afternoons sometimes, I would get away and go down the street to sit and watch all the boats go up and down the Pasic River. Sitting there, I would think about everything that had happened since I had joined the Army, almost five months before, and wonder why I had not heard from home. It was getting close to December 1st, my 17ᵗʰ birthday (my *real* birthday), and still I had heard nothing. I guess I could understand my family's silence, since I was the one who had run away in the first place.

As luck would have it, our Bataan detail was to pull out the last day of November 1941, which meant that I would be in Bataan on my birthday and miss the party Nelda had planned for me. When I told her we were leaving, she broke down and sobbed.

Though no one knew precisely where it came from, a cloud of uncertainty—or maybe apprehension—seemed to be hovering around us. We could not quite define it, but for some reason, it was extra hard to say goodbye that morning as we pulled out of Manila. It was a pretty day, and looking at the road lined by the waving and always-smiling natives, I again thought how good they had always been for our morale. Every time I would toot the horn, it seemed as everyone, including the older folks, would wave at me. They were such happy-go-lucky people, you couldn't help but like them. If you so much as said a simple "Hey there," they would take you home with them for dinner.

Hours later, when we arrived in Bataan, we were told that it would take us at least two weeks to handle all the ammo that had been delivered: 500-pound bombs, 30-pound fragment bombs, and—something we hadn't had in Bataan before—100-pound bombs. Most of our ammo had been shells, 155 and 75 mm, so needless to say, we were surprised and somewhat unnerved by the delivery.

Meanwhile, it was, as usual, hard work every day, from sunrise to sundown. At night in camp, we would play cards, or sit around and tell stories and jokes, or talk about our families and friends back home. Many of the guys would often kid me about being from Alabama. I would always come back saying, "Y'all know, it's the number-one state." That would get a big rah-rah. "Well," I said, "look at any list of the states. Ain't Alabama always the first one?"

We had been in Bataan for a week, and as we sat in that jungle camp kidding each other and swapping stories deep into the night, we had no way to know that the next day our lives would be changed—forever.

3

WAR

The morning was like any other: time to get up, get dressed, go to work. It was December 8th in the Philippines. In Hawaii, it was Sunday, December 7th, 1941—"a date which will live in infamy."

I was getting my big truck ready to roll out when all of a sudden, I heard a lot of yelling in the midst of a great commotion. Sergeant Debouch was shouting for everyone to come immediately to the orderly room, and Sergeant Mahoney was beating the chow bell with an urgency I hadn't heard before. We knew there must be something big happening and took off running to see what it was.

After we were all inside and the noise had died down a little, we were informed that the Japanese had just bombed Pearl Harbor and were expected to attack the Philippine Islands at any moment. Our first job was to report to the docks, pick up the ammunition there, transport it to our warehouses, and then check regularly for any change in orders.

Within minutes, I was sitting on the dock waiting to have ammo loaded onto my truck. Confused and worried, I was trying to understand what was really happening. *Are we all going to be involved in a full-blown war with Japan?* I didn't think it was really possible. As my mind raced from one thought to another, I reflected on my entire past and present. Of all the places in the world I could be, I figured, right here, in the Philippines was the worst. *Why had I chosen to come here?* I thought about the Marouka Bar fight with the Japanese sailors and wished we had killed all of them. The gall. *How could those Japs dare start a war with the United States?!*

We really hustled. Everyone—everyone was scared. We were afraid of being bombed. We were afraid of being killed. So we worked even harder, making trips back and forth, back and forth to the docks all morning, trying to keep our fears in check. We had to get all the barges unloaded before the bombing started.

Around one o'clock in the afternoon, the first air raid sirens sounded off on Corregidor in Manila Bay. We all raced to the clearing at Little Baguio, from which we could see all the way across the bay to Manila.

They were here. Speechless, we watched the Japanese planes invading in precise V formations as they flew over the city. The first bombs hit Nichols Field, and then a formation of planes hit Cavite Naval Station. As they flew past us, they dropped bombs on Corregidor. When the anti-aircraft shells exploded, it blew one of the Jap planes to bits before our very eyes. Cheers burst out as our emotions swirled. We then looked at each other, and a sinking realization came over us—the war really *had* started, and we were part of it!

We hurried back to our camp as the all-clear sounded and waited for further orders. At the same time, we wondered, *Why aren't our P-40 fighters in the air by now engaging the Japs? And where the heck are the B-17s? What in the world is happening?* The Jap planes flew around like they owned the place, with absolutely no interference from our side. Everyone was wondering out loud. Some of the guys were ready to go back to Manila to hunt and cut down every last single Jap. As the day went on, though, we continued to watch helplessly as more waves of bombers hit Clark Field, and Subic Bay, and then Nichols Field, and Cavite Naval Station…and then Corregidor. We weren't sure what other targets had been hit, but we knew it wasn't good. With the Japanese flying around wherever they wanted, and with no opposition—we were in desperate trouble.

Sergeant Debouch then came and chose about 36 of us to serve as a special convoy, taking bombs to Nichols Field—on the other side of Manila from where we were based. We were told that if another air attack began, we were to break up the convoy and each truck was to find its own way to the field. That way, it was more likely that some of us would get through; a single truck was a harder target to hit than a whole convoy.

With even more urgency, we loaded our trucks. Each truck flew the red flag that meant we had full priority over all other traffic on the road, and each truck was manned with a relief driver and a guard on top armed with a BAR (Browning Automatic Rifle) to look out for planes and handle any other problems that might come up. Our orders were to drive faster than normal and in close order, and not to allow any other cars or trucks between us. When we arrived in Manila, we were not to stop at any red lights, but were to flash our lights, blow horns, and keep moving, even if an air raid was in progress.

As we raced through the villages where we normally traveled, the kids were out. Everyone was yelling and waving victory signs at us, celebrating and cheering us on. Yet at the same time, they became confused and could not understand why we didn't stop at places where we had normally taken breaks before. Of course there was no time to explain.

As we approached Manila, the air raid sirens began to blare again. We closed up our ranks even tighter and drove on. Anti-aircraft shells were exploding overhead. We could hear screams, sounds of people running, and whistles blowing. The war was on. And the Filipinos were going wild.

Unbelievably, the gate guards at Nichols Field had problems obtaining clearance for us to enter in. We argued that we needed to get in and get out before another raid. But it wasn't until around midnight that we were finally allowed onto the base and were told where to unload. Before we were finished unloading and off the base, though, another air raid alarm sounded! Each truck dashed to the back side of the field and waited. There we watched as the Japanese planes came in and hit some of the hangers and a runway just a short distance from our position. What a helpless feeling. The sickening sound of a bomb aimed down toward you, then the movement of the earth below you. My heart would almost stop as I held my breath until the bomb exploded on target. When I was able to hear that awful thud against the target and the noise rebounding off the ground, I knew that I was alive for at least a little while longer. I must have been praying, but I can't remember anything except watching the horrible destruction all around me. This was the first time in my life where I couldn't grasp the visible reality of what was happening right in front of my eyes.

As I noticed some of our planes that had been destroyed earlier that day, I still couldn't come to grips with why our troops had just let them sit there. We had been warned that the Japs were coming; in fact, after we heard about Pearl Harbor, we had hours to prepare before the first Japanese bombs hit the Philippines. *Why were we hit like sitting ducks just waiting for it to happen?* I asked over and over. No one knew the answer.

As the all-clear sounded, our trucks rolled out and returned to our company compound. But then, we found it locked up tight—all bases were in high security mode. As we pulled into our motor pool area, all of a sudden, the air raid sirens went off again. We made it to our company quarters, where we had .50 caliber machine guns on top of the wall. As the planes flew far above us, we could hear the machine guns going off and see tracer bullets forming red streaks everywhere.

When we ran out in the courtyard, we could see one of our men on top of the wall. He had totally freaked out and was rocking from side to side holding one of the .50 caliber machine guns. He was a wild man, shooting everywhere—over the river, over the tops of buildings, into our quarters and compound, and down the street. It was obvious that he was out of control. Sergeant Smith had to climb up the ladder and knock him off the wall to get him to stop! Unfortunately, the destruction caused by his actions was worse than the wreckage caused by the Japanese bombings.

It was now 3:30 a.m. No one in our group had rested or had any sleep since the night before. Our master sergeant then made us some food and we were ordered to get some rest. Later that morning I woke up to find that Nelda was downstairs waiting for me. I was also told that this would be the last time she could come to the compound. No visitors would be allowed from this point on, and all leaves were canceled.

Nelda had also been informed, and when I got downstairs, she was crying. As I walked up to her, she grabbed me, crying as hard as she could and holding on to me, telling me how much she loved me and that she just had to go with me. Sergeant Warren had to pull her away from me and ask her to leave. Then she started to yell at me for not understanding how much she loved me. In an attempt to calm her down, I promised that I would come to see her. When she finally left, I knew there was a strong probability that I would never see her again. No one had ever cared for me in the same way Nelda had, and it was hard for me to understand her love.

That day, we received orders to return to Bataan. But first, we had to go to Fort William McKinley and load supplies to take with us. Immediately, 18 of our men who had been jailed in the brig were released by Sergeant Warren at the orders of the commanding officer so that they could help in the fight. In spite of most of Manila being in disarray, our company was very well organized.

I could sense the special feelings towards us by Sergeants Warren and Debouch, and also a friendlier attitude extended to us by the officers who had not been involved with us much before. The seven of us who had come over from the States together had been accepted into the company. Most of us weren't heavy drinkers and were reliable at work. Our friends and coworkers had respected us for a job well done.

By this time, I had made corporal because I had been attending school. Usually, ranks in our company were slow to achieve because someone had to retire or go back to the States before anyone could be promoted. All these restrictions were gone now that the war was on; there was no retirement or returning to the States for any of us.

We went to load our trucks and wanted to get back to Bataan as quickly as possible. Our trip was long, and was basically uneventful, except for a couple more air raids. It made my blood boil when I passed by houses that had been destroyed by the bombings in the last several hours. And then, I saw a tiny baby blown up into a tree—that was especially hard to deal with. Our world had been turned upside down. The island paradise that we had enjoyed had changed into a living hell, especially for the Filipino people who lived there. They didn't know what to expect. They were all trying to be helpful, but what could they do? This was war. Rumors were going wild: "The Japs have taken Hawaii…they're invading the U.S. West Coast…they've landed north of Los Angeles…they'll be landing troops on one of our beaches tomorrow…" No one could tell us for sure what was happening, and no one knew what to believe. There was confusion everywhere.

As soon as we got to Bataan, we were told that we were not to have anything to do with anyone we didn't know; we were not to tell anyone where we were based or anything about our operation. Nothing. Absolutely nothing. We were also informed that the war plans called for all U.S. troops to retreat to Bataan in order to make a stand there, if necessary. Though we tried not to show it, we were depressed and afraid at heart, but had no time to dwell on our fear.

Thirty-two men were chosen to help set up field depots as close to the front lines as possible and to keep them supplied with ammunition. We were also expected to supply the air bases with bombs and other ammo as needed. We were given instructions on how to build a secure ammo dump and how to dispose of it in case the ammo couldn't be removed before a retreat had to be made.

The air raids had now become regular occurrences, and at this point, we had a pretty good idea where the next bombs would land and when and where to hide in case of a raid. There was some relief as we watched the planes passing over us, knowing they would hit other targets instead of us. But this wasn't always the case. At one point, enemy planes invaded Clark Field while we were still there waiting to unload. We had no time to take cover as bombs were fired, and some exploded within ten feet of us. The falling flack from the anti-aircraft shells being shot was just as bad or worse. It made my gut hurt that I had to lie there knowing there was next to nothing I could do to keep my truck and ammo safe, and the crew and myself alive.

The air units were so confused that we were unable to find any-one who could tell us where to unload our 500-pound bombs. I figured that as soon as the all-clear sounded, we would dump them close to a hangar that had not sustained too much damage...but we would need special equipment to unload these massive bombs... and there was none to be found. So we decided that each truck would simply let the tailgate down; we would back up as fast as pos-sible, and then the driver would slam on the brakes. Consequently, the bombs would roll out on the ground, with some bombs drop-ping right on top of the others. We then decided to put the boxes of fuses on top of one pile. This "fast unload" process allowed us to leave before another bombing raid came over.

Now we were on our way back to Bataan, and all too soon we were caught unaware by two Jap dive bombers who had come in from behind us. Luckily, we were close to a large, wooded area. We immediately drove into the jungle and were able to get all but two trucks off the road into the woods. As we moved the trucks around, the planes kept coming back, and so, those two trucks that remained on the road were damaged badly. We had to leave one truck behind. Fortunately, all the trucks were empty, and none of the men were hurt, just really shook up. This would be the beginning of the attacks against the ammo trucks, and we would become one of their prime targets. In spite of this, of the 32 men that we started with, only three asked to be relieved of duty from these trips.

I had been raised in a religious home. I knew what was right and what was wrong. And when I had considered joining the Army, I would sometimes wonder how I would ever be able to kill anyone on purpose. But after seeing how these savage Japs unmercifully bombed the people in Manila and especially after seeing that little baby blown into a tree, my anger was pushed to the limit. This was also the first time I witnessed how other men reacted under extreme pressure—some with a controlled type of reason, others with emotions gone amok, some with a semblance of courage, and others with irrational behavior. I understood immediately that if I expected to get through this dreadful ordeal, I would have to kill when the time came without giving the action any thought, or feeling any regret.

The next day, a friend and I walked up to the Little Bagiuo Hospital, just a short distance from our company area. When we had returned to Bataan, they had opened this hospital, a quarter mile from General Wainwright's hospital. As we approached one of the large crosses located at a corner of the hospital, a Jap dive bomber came in low, dropped his bombs, and strafed the entire area a couple of times. One of the bombs dropped right next to the white cross. I went into the ditch on the right side of the road, and my friend went into another ditch on the left side. As the plane turned, I could see the Jap pilot look back, as if he was gloating. I could have grabbed the plane with my bare hands and crushed that scum to the earth. That pilot's blatant disregard for the injured in the hospital was like spitting in my face.

I then turned to look for my friend and say something…but…but…I kept turning around. A few seconds later, I noticed a bomb had hit on the left side where he had been lying. I walked over… and saw a shoe. I bent down to pick it up…his foot was still in it. That was all I ever found of him. For a minute, I didn't breathe, and there was this indescribable pain. And then, the next minute I became enraged.

That was the turning point for me. Those barbaric animals did not care who or what they hit. Hatred took control of me, it consumed me, and I wanted to kill every Jap I could lay my hands on. There was no more fear of injury. There was no more fear of dying. All fears were completely and totally obliterated. And in their place was a deadly calm. Now, it would be about surviving and surviving to enact revenge. I wanted to see a Jap I could kill and then do it without any feeling at all. This was "K" day—"Kill the Japs Day."

About the time of the second air raid in Bataan, we had noticed that right before the planes approached, the monkeys would start running and screaming in the trees. Sergeant Mahoney, our mess sergeant, had been sitting at a table and heard a monkey screaming. When he looked up, a small monkey jumped up on the table, where he sat shaking and squealing. When the bombs hit Corregidor, the monkey ran under a chair and hid there, all the while continuing to shriek.

This same little monkey took up with us later. He could tell when the planes coming over were Japanese planes. A few of our P-40s would fly over, and he would remain calm, but when the Japanese planes came, he would start to sound the alarm and even beat you to the foxhole. We called him "Radar." He stayed with us until we had to surrender.

Our crew of 32 was now down to 29, and Colonel Hurst called us into a meeting to tell us what he expected of us as a working unit on the advanced ammo dumps. We were to report all air raids against the trucks and not to put any man at risk to save equipment. He told us how important it was to position an ammo dump so that aircraft could not see it. It was also important, he told us, that the supplies could be moved easily in case the lines moved back or changed.

If we had to get help at any time from the natives or other persons, we were given work slips to pay for the labor, which were backed by the U.S. government. If for any reason a man was wounded, we were to try to get him to the nearest medical corps unit. If anyone was killed, he suggested we bring their body back to the field hospital, or if we had to leave the body, make a record of where the body had been left, time of death, and any other information.

If for any reason we had to have transportation to return to headquarters, we were to take any car or truck we could find and give the owner a voucher so they could collect compensation from our government. In particular, we were not to tell anything to anyone about our unit or where the headquarters was located. No one, regardless of his rank, was to stop us from going where we were ordered to go. We were to tell them to contact Colonel Hurst at the 75th Ordinance Company to confirm our orders.

The Japanese were stepping up the number of air raids all over the place, and there were reports of their naval ships just off the coast. We had received specific reports of small Japanese landing forces in several places on northern Luzon Island, and other landings were expected to take place any day. Under immense stress, we still could not come to grips with the confusion and continued to ask ourselves, *Where are more of our P-40s? Why aren't they trying to stop these formations of Jap bombers?* We weren't aware that virtually all our interceptors had been destroyed on the first day, so these questions still remained at the front of our minds.

We were now in the second week of air attacks on all major airfields, Army posts, and naval stations. In addition, our trucks were under heavy attack every day. Our loss was small; even so, most guys were afraid to go out during the day. That meant that most of our trips to Manila were at night. By the end of the third week, our group was down to two men—Gerald Block and me. Some simply refused to go out at any time. And a couple other men joined units at the front line...we never heard from them again.

Even in the midst of the devastation and horror, there was still humor to be found. The engineers had been ordered to paint all cars, trucks, and equipment green—G.I. olive drab green. They were to stop traffic and paint any car on the road, including windows and anything else on the vehicle that would shine or reflect light. In the meantime, a Navy captain reported to General Wainwright's headquarters, driving up in a 1942 black Buick Roadmaster that had just come in from the States. The car was slick and shiny—probably still smelled new inside. The captain proceeded into the headquarters building for a while; and when he came out, he stopped, looked around, but could not find his nice black Buick anywhere. A sergeant for the engineers company was standing there, so the captain went up to him and asked, "Where is my Buick car? I left it out here." "It's over there, Captain," replied the sergeant, pointing to some Army trucks and cars. "Right where you left it, Sir."

"I don't see it, Sergeant," was his reply. "It's there all right." At that point the captain noticed what looked like a Buick automobile. He also realized his car was now G.I. green.

"On whose orders did you do this to my new car!?" the captain shouted angrily.

"Orders from USAFFE Headquarters, Sir."

The captain rushed back into General Wainwright's headquarters. Loud words came out from the building, and soon the captain marched back outside. No sooner had he come out than he did an about-face and marched right back in again. And then again, he came back out hollering about how in the tarnation they could do such a thing to his brand-new Buick. When he got close to the car, he realized his windshield, all the windows, headlights, shiny chrome, and whitewall tires were all painted the GI olive drab, too. Holding the door open to see the road, he sped out of the drive, slinging gravel all over the place.

The sergeant turned around to see a small audience witnessing the most recent drama. Slightly shrugging his shoulders, he remarked, "Just following orders. You can't please everyone." We all needed this light reprieve. Even among all the terror and ruin of our simple paradise, we were trying to make the best of it.

The Filipino people were also trying to cope with the loss of life and property due to the air raids and were bracing for an even worse predicament—the Japanese invasion they knew was coming. About the 20th of December, approximately two weeks after the first attack, we were informed that the Jap ships were offshore and were making plans to attack our main force at Lingayen Bay. The few aircraft we had left attempted to hit the invasion force but did little damage. If our planes had been in the air on the 8th of December instead of on the ground, the invasion of the 14th Japanese Army could have been delayed or even entirely prevented. Our B-17 fleet could have taken off shortly after we were told Pearl Harbor had been hit and bombed the Japanese planes on the ground on Formosa. All I could do was keep asking... *Why?*

When the 14th Japanese Army came ashore at Lingayen Bay, they were met by Filipino Army troops who were poorly trained and ill-equipped. It was an easy landing for the Japanese forces and extremely disheartening for the Filipino people. In some locations there was no resistance at all. I arrived near the front on the third day after the invasion, and was to set up an ammo dump. Someone had loaded blank ammo from Fort William McKinley, not knowing the difference, and now, over 80 percent of the Filipino Army men were shooting it.

By the time we had a small ammo dump set up, however, the Japs were too close for us to even try to blow it up and keep it from them. I was lucky to get my crew and empty trucks out before the area was overrun. Miles down the road, I would see Filipino Army men walking away from the action. When we stopped to ask where the rest of their company was, most of the men answered that they didn't know.

The Japs moved south quickly, and USAFFE (United States Army Forces in the Far East) gave orders to move back into Bataan. However, the attempt to retreat was a total disaster. There was only one main road, and it was jammed bumper to bumper. Our troops and equipment were like sitting ducks for the Jap planes, which had a field day. A statement that came out of USAFFE reported that the delay to order withdrawal back into Bataan had been caused by General MacArthur who was waiting to determine the intentions of the invading Japanese forces. Believe me, when the Japanese 14th Army, one of their best, had landed and was moving fast toward Manila, it did not take a military genius to figure out what their intentions were.

The road into Bataan was closed by the Japs on the first or second of January 1942, cutting off many Americans, Philippine scouts, and the Philippine Army, not to mention food, medical supplies, and equipment. The USAFFE had forbidden the tons of food on hand be moved to Bataan. Then, the USAFFE allowed over 30,000 old men, women and children, who were depending on the Army to feed them, to move back into Bataan, where there would soon be little or nothing to eat.

General MacArthur notified Washington that the retreat was "complete and successful." The truth was that we were short on rations from the very beginning. Every living thing around—monkeys, armadillos, cats, dogs, even grubs—that could be eaten was killed by the men on Bataan and used for food.

As the first line of defense was drawn up by the Americans and Philippines, the Japanese came upon stiff resistance from forces under General Wainwright's command. We knew it was going to get harder to hold them off, and as the overwhelming Jap forces came against us, turning our flanks, we were forced to move back farther again and again, until we were finally back as far as we could go.

The detail to set up ammo dumps close to the front lines was reduced to only two men out of our original 32. These two men were my working partner, Gerald, and me. We lost the guards who rode on top of all the trucks, and had to depend on Filipino men we were able to pick up on our way to help unload at the dumps. Many times we had to do it alone, or with the help of the Army units close to the front lines.

We found ourselves between the battle lines at least 20 times, and had to fight our own way out. Our ammo dumps had been wired to blow up at the time we set them up. When we saw that we were going to lose a dump, I would order all drivers and helpers back. Gerald and I would lie in wait until the Japs were on the dump looking at their captured supplies, then we would blow the dump and them to kingdom come.

In one instance, we had five railroad boxcars half loaded with 155 black powder containers used as charges in the big guns. We waited in the bushes until about 50 Jap soldiers were all over the boxcars, checking out the contents. When we blew up the five boxcars, the Jap soldiers were blown as high as 50 to 60 feet in the air, killing all who were standing on the boxcars and delaying their advance. A blast of machine gunfire came our way, but fortunately we were not hit. In the midst of all the death so far, I still would not allow myself to be overcome by emotion for our loss; neither could I feel anything but satisfaction for the enemy's failures. Even so, I couldn't celebrate just yet, for the present deathly and horrid atmosphere would prove to be minor compared to what was to come.

Three weeks after the road to Bataan had been closed by the Japs, I was on my way back from the west front on January 23, 1942, when the Japanese made a push where the front was closest to the central mountain. They had also sent a landing party to the end of the Bataan Peninsula. The fight that took place there was named "Battle of the Points." The Japs' original plan was to take Bataan by the first of February 1942, and they were right on schedule.

I was driving along the road around the southwest end of Bataan when I saw a United States major beside the road waving his arms for me to stop, so I pulled over. He said that he knew that we were an ordinance detail by the look of our trucks and wanted to know what we had on board that would help him and his small force fight the Japanese who had landed below his position on the beach at Agloloma Point. It was discouraging to find out that all he had were rifles and a navy anti-aircraft gun that was set at a 90-degree upward angle to shoot at aircraft. They had tried to tie it to a tree to shoot down off the bluff that surrounded the beach and at the Japs below. Each time they would shoot it though, the recoil would knock the gun off the tree and they would have to start all over again.

There were an estimated 6,000 enemy troops down there, and if we didn't do something, the major said, they would soon climb the bluff, take the highway, and cut off communications between the eastern and western sides of our defense perimeter.

I asked the major where he came from in the USA, and he told me, Kansas. I asked if he knew what a hog watering or feeding trough was.

"What the hell does that have to do with this situation?" he asked.

I told him we had three warehouses full of 30-pound fragmentation bombs that we could slide down on the Japanese beachhead using the same V-shaped trough-like structures that we used to slop the hogs back home. One end of the troughs would be set next to a tree where we could tie off the arming wire to set the fuse and then slide the bombs down the chutes. The other end of the troughs would extend out over the edge of the bluff and over the location of the Japs.

He told me to go get the bombs and that they would build the chutes. I went to headquarters and talked to Colonel Hurst, outlining my plan. When Colonel Hurst approved my idea, I loaded up three truckloads of bombs, fuses, and arming wires, and hustled back to Agloloma Point. When I got there, they had 17 chutes ready to slide the bombs down onto the Japanese beachhead, and we went to work.

Some bombs hit rocks, weeds, and tree limbs, but even then the rocks rained down on the forces below. Other bombs hit the target right-on! By the time we had used up two truckloads of bombs, we could no longer hear any sounds coming up from below. After waiting a little longer, we decided to go ahead and dump the rest of the three truckloads down on them. Ultimately, we killed most of them. From their own records, they reported that their beachhead attempt failed completely.

I later read the following passage in official accounts of the Bataan campaign: "General MacArthur's G-2, on a staff visit to I Corps…became involved in [the Battle of the Points]. When all United States officers became casualties, he took command of the 1st Philippine Constabulary, defending Agloloma Point and reestablished the position by a sharp counterattack." When I read this account, I realized that the writer was talking about the major, me, my hog troughs, and three truckloads of jerry-rigged fragmentation bombs. I have often wondered if that major was the visiting G-2 from headquarters.

Some Japs did manage to climb up the side of the bluff. And the Philippine Army and other Americans who were there went hand-to-hand with them. I was walking down to one end of the bluff to see how things were going when a Jap soldier jumped out in front of me. They didn't like to shoot at close range because in doing so, they would give away their location; they were supposed to use their bayonets. He lunged at me before I could get my gun into position. I stepped aside from his bayonet, but it caught my rifle strap holder and knocked my rifle out of my hand.

As he came up next to me, I grabbed him around the neck and pulled out the knife that Nelda's brother had made for me. I stuck it all the way through him, nicking my own chest. I threw his body over the side of the bluff with the thought that just in case he was not dead, the drop of about 400 feet would finish him off. As the fighting died down, I could not find the major again, so I, along with two Filipino men who had come with me to help unload, went back to headquarters. I reported the details of the bombings and the fight to Colonel Hurst, and he concluded that we might have managed to save Bataan until the long-promised reinforcements could arrive. He called his administrative officer, Major Potter, and told him to submit the necessary paperwork so that I would receive the Medal of Honor for my actions. This battle was the first defeat the Japs had suffered since they started the war. The Battle of the Points, as it was called, provided Bataan two more months to wait for help. I consider this one of the most important engagements in the Pacific at that time, and I was proud to have played a part.

The time it took Japan to pull back some of its forces from the South Pacific helped save Australia from invasion, thereby shortening the war by a year. If the attempted Japanese landing had been successful, their push on land on our west flank would have linked up with the Algoloma Point landing. This would have cut our supply line to the west front, and Bataan would have fallen within a few days. Then the Japanese would have had only Corregidor to take and the Philippine campaign would have been complete. In the end, Corregidor held up for only 23 days after Bataan fell.

If Corregidor had been taken earlier, MacArthur would not have made it to Australia and would have been captured.

When it got down to the facts of holding Bataan, the job was to fight with no restrictions. The officers and men showed what they were made of and the spirit they had to hold off the forces that vastly outnumbered them from the very beginning. General McArthur passed command to General Wainwright, who had little to work with. Pushed back against the China Sea with orders to fight to the last man, what could he do except pick up whatever pieces were left?

/ The propaganda from the radio station finally stopped. We were no longer expecting anything from anyone. General King—who I think was a great general—was faced with a bigger problem. He had inherited an order to do the impossible—hold off longer at a great cost of life, or decide just when and how to get out of this dilemma. The facts were right there before him. He was faced with starving civilians in a camp that was formed for the women and children caught up in the retreat back to Bataan. The soldiers who were trying to fight were sick and worn out from enduring the horrors. The front line smelled from one end to the other with the stench of dead men. Jap bodies lay everywhere. No one wanted to bury them. Helping the wounded back to a corpsman so they could be taken to the hospital was almost impossible. Some wounded were never moved from where they fell, because the fighting would not permit it.

During this time, I scarcely had a chance to visit Nelda in the civilian camp and help her however I could. Every minute was consumed with delivering needed ammo to the men. Nelda, too, was getting desperate for food, the same as the others in the camp. Although she thought she could be of help to others, she was restricted as to where she could go. When I looked at the women and children, I knew that the same questions were on their minds: "Will we be safe here? Is any help coming?" As in other places, optimistic rumors would eventually prove to be false, which became very discouraging.

Even so, there wasn't much time for any thoughts of hope. Actually, there wasn't even time to think about what might happen tomorrow or even in a few hours. I was just barely holding onto life and body. When I did have a few moments to be still and think, my thoughts would drift to my family and my girl back home and wonder if I would ever make it back. I guess that's when a little wishful thinking would enter my mind. Sometimes I would think about places I had gone and the things I had done, and there would be a question as to whether I had done right or wrong. Yet still, there was no time to agonize over the past.

Now, in the middle of such hideous and dreadful surroundings, my anger would still sometimes take the place of reasoning, as it did when I was on the front line and the fighting was ferocious. The Philippine Army had captured about 40 Jap soldiers; and Gerald and I were the only Americans present. They asked us what to do with them. I sharply said to the sergeant in charge, "Are you going to feed them or take care of them?"

He looked back at me and said, "That's what I want you to do—take them back to a prison camp. I do not know of one."

My quick suggestion was that since food was so short, he could take them down the road a ways and let them escape. I then asked him if he knew what to do when prisoners tried to escape. The sergeant slightly smiled, and with a look of understanding, ordered his men to march the Japs down the road. Soon we heard a slew of shots. When they came back, he shrugged at me and said, "The prisoners tried to escape."

Throughout the ordeal, our orders were not to stop the ammo truck for anything and to keep rolling. However, one night there was a serious accident involving an ambulance going back to the hospital with wounded men. As I went to pass by, I saw Jolly, a man

I knew, lying on the road, with part of the ambulance resting on top of his arm. This time, I had to stop. We took the truck winch and lifted the wrecked ambulance to release him. I later learned that he lost his arm, but I was grateful that he did not have to lie there and bleed to death.

On another occasion, we were ordered to go to the front lines, but when we got there, the place had already fallen into Japanese hands. Before we knew it, our six Corbitt trucks were surrounded by Japs. My truck was the lead truck and Gerald's was in the rear. When I saw what was happening, I blew the loud air horn on my truck, the next one blew his horn, and so on down the line.

For a moment, the loud noise stunned and disoriented the Japs. Taking advantage of the confusion, I bailed out of my truck, ran back to the next truck, and jumped on the side. The other trucks started backing up. The Japs then started shooting and the relief drivers returned the fire. Our plan was working. Each truck turned at the same time except Gerald's. He started shooting at the truck I had just abandoned. It was loaded with 155 big-gun black-powder charges. When he hit those canisters, the truck blew to pieces. One of our relief drivers was killed, and we lost the truck I was driving; the rest of us were able to escape.

The explosion of my truck gave us time to get back down the road. About three miles back, we came upon the Philippine Army unit, who had given us a signal that they were in retreat. Their ammo was short, the Japs had been moving in from the side, and the front line had collapsed. So they had to get out with their big gun as quickly as they could. By that time, though, the big gun was about ten miles down the road behind us. There were so few of the big 155s that we did everything we could to save them, and fortunately, we were able to retrieve that one.

In the meantime, another request came in to repair a 155 gun for a Philippine scouting company close to the front lines. The company was located on a mountain point close to a road intersection and command post overlooking a valley where the Japs were advancing. It was an absolute must to save that gun and the command lookout, too, if possible. By the time Gerald and I arrived at the location, the top of the hill had changed hands three times. We had the parts to fix the gun, but we had to wait for the Philippine scouts to take back the top of the mountain so we could get down the road to where the big gun was located.

Heavy fighting raged all night. By daybreak there was a lull, and we got word to move out. I was driving the big Corbitt truck and had the big gun in tow. Gerald and I were prepared. Four BARs had been loaded with 30 round clips. In addition to the BARs, we had three or four Springfield rifles and our .45 pistols, plus dozens of hand grenades. Our windshield was opened out, and all the windows were down. We had been warned that the Japs were close to the intersection.

As we approached the three-road intersection, there in front of us was a Jap setting up a tripod machine gun. Gerald took a BAR and emptied the 30-round clip into the Jap, just blowing him to pieces. As this happened, we were turning right to go down the mountain road, which had five switchback curves. The Philippine troops were on the right side of the road, and the Japs were on the left. We found ourselves taking heavy gunfire from both sides.

All of a sudden, Gerald yelled that another Jap soldier was in the middle of the road. Gerald fired and the Jap jumped in the ditch. I had the truck accelerator slammed to the floor. The first curve was an inside curve, and as I looked in the side mirror I could see the long gun barrel scraping the inside bank of the mountain. On the next curve, the wheels of the trailer were half off the side of the mountain. The Jap who had been in the road was now in the next inside curve. The gun barrel got him as he tried to get away.

Gunshots were so close you could feel the concussion against your ears. We went down and around the next two zigzag curves at full speed. As we leveled off at the bottom, we saw the Philippine scouts' checkpoint up ahead where we were to leave the gun, and we kept moving full speed ahead!

I thought the gas pedal was stuck until Gerald kicked my foot off of it. I was frozen to the accelerator with only one thought in mind—to get down the mountain and get the gun in place. As we came to a gradual stop, the scouts came out, chasing after us to retrieve the gun.

When we got out of the truck, we counted 32 bullet holes in the cab. Yet neither Gerald nor I had one scratch on us. There had to have been angels there to protect us. There was no other reasonable explanation. We continued on to headquarters where even more men surveyed the damage to the truck. No one could believe we had been in that truck and survived.

Other miracles would happen. A few nights later, I was returning to headquarters with our crew and a convoy of about eight trucks. And once again, I was the lead truck. We were in the foothills, and there was a drop of about 300 feet on the outside of the road. As I came into a curve, a jeep came around the curve toward us at a high speed. I had the truck door open with one foot on the running board and the other on the gas pedal. In trying to miss the jeep, my left front wheel hit a washout on the side of the road and my truck flipped over. The door served as a lever that threw the truck over the side of the mountain down 300 feet. I fell out and that truck flipped right over me, leaving me at the edge of the bluff without a scratch.

While we were assigned on other trips, Jap snipers would often hide behind our lines and place themselves in a tree so they could see as much of the road as possible and then attack our vehicles or soldiers passing by. Our ammo trucks were always considered a top target; accordingly, we were always on the lookout for these snipers. Many times they would shoot out a windshield or kill one of our drivers. It came about that a 155 big gun on our west China Sea front needed a part. So, traveling in a jeep, a Filipino relief driver went along with me to go repair the gun. When we traveled on any such type of job, we flew a big red flag. Unfortunately, it also gave blatant notice to any sniper that our jeep was on an important mission.

It was late afternoon when we rounded a curve, and the next thing we knew, a sniper had blasted out our windshield with a burst of shots. The next second, I jerked the jeep into the left ditch and immediately dove out along the side of the jeep. Right away, my nose and lungs were filled with a powder dust. I could barely breathe but managed to crawl up on the bank next to the jeep in order to hide from the sniper. The Jap must have thought we were dead, because all was quiet for about the next 15 minutes. Then I heard a truck coming, and I immediately decided that I had to alert whoever was approaching. So I quickly crawled back in the ditch and kept crawling along, staying in the ditch, until I thought the sniper would not be able to see me. I was able to warn a Filipino scout just in time that a sniper was up ahead. As he stopped, I told him to stay there and also stop anyone else who came up behind him. He told me he knew for sure there were some men a short distance back down the road. So he ran back and brought about six other men with him. We decided to try to find the sniper.

I told all these men the purpose of my mission, and we all agreed that we had to find this Jap and get me on my way. They tossed me a Springfield rifle, and we spread out in different directions. We were running out of time. It was getting dark, and we knew if we didn't get him soon, it would be too late to try.

For a little while, everything remained quiet. Then another group of men came walking down the road toward my jeep from a different direction. A sudden burst of gunfire came from a nearby tree directed toward those men. Three of us closest to that tree immediately opened fire, followed by the fire of two other men. We saw movement in the tree, and then another blast of gunfire came from the tree. Perfect—that gave us his exact location. All seven of us simultaneously fired into the tree, and the sniper fell out. One of the scouts ran up to make sure he was dead and grabbed his gun.

When I returned to my jeep, I found my relief driver had been shot and was dead. One of the men who had been walking down the road was also dead, and another had been shot in the leg. There was almost always a great sacrifice that was made. Up to this point, however, I had experienced little injury. Even when I was trapped between the lines and was hit by shell fragments in my right side, I was quickly attended to by a Filipino corpsman who was able to remove a piece of steel and patch me up. There was no one to drive my truck, so I drove back to headquarters and never did find time to go to the field hospital.

The overall situation was becoming more than desperate. The food rations for all troops on Bataan were cut to less than half. One can of salmon and some rice was what approximately 30 men were eating. By this time, all the horses, water buffalo, monkeys, snakes, and lizards had been eaten, even wild boars and any other animal we could catch. The iodine used to put into contaminated water so that it would be safe to drink was about gone. Malaria was rampant. When I would go to the front lines, I found that the men were hungry, their clothes in rags, their hearts broken, and their morale low. It was devastating.

Shortwave radio would pick up the "Voice of America." I can still hear them saying, "Good morning, fellow Americans" or "Good Morning, Mr. and Mrs. America…The rocky walls of Bataan still stand this morning. The battle-weary Americans and Filipino troops still hold against overwhelming odds. The full force of the powerful Imperial Japanese Army has been unable to break the lines of these brave fighting men. General McArthur expects the forces in Bataan will hold out until reinforcements arrive."

Then we would turn to another station to hear what Tokyo Rose had to say about the report from the Voice of America in San Francisco. She would say something like, "Good morning, Boys. You know help is not on the way. Well, we have something for you today. The Imperial Japanese Army has your menu ready for you. It's time you raise your white flag and come over to us and get some clean clothes, good food, and good music. The Americans do not care about you. There is no way to win."

She would continue, "The 14th Army has this planned for you today. At dawn this morning, the shelling began in the Moran area. Bombing and strafing will continue all day. Shelling will be done all up and down the front lines. Now why do you want to stay there and get killed or injured when you could be safe by simply coming across our lines? We will see that you are treated well. Now here is some music to help you remember your friends and family back home."

Can you imagine what this did to us poor dogfaces who were nailed down, fighting a disheartening battle, struggling with all types of horrid sicknesses, starving for food, filthy with no way to wash, and then having to listen to people who were safe and sound, siccing the big dog on us. I felt like everyone else. *Why are we here in these grim circumstances while even our own people are making it worse?* The radio station on Corregidor was broadcasting some other mess that sure didn't help us either. They did not impress or mislead the Japs in any way. The Japs weren't stupid; they knew how things really were on Bataan. We poor suckers who were on the front lines had nothing but a blue sky overhead, not even the protection of a big tunnel like most of the men on Corregidor.

The final weeks and days on Bataan were brutal. Some men were so sick they could not even hold their own heads up, yet they were expected to hold the line against the enemy. Their patrols were testing our lines every chance they could, day and night, and the shells kept coming in.

Then the radio station at Corregidor broadcasted this interview:

Q. "Good morning, Sergeant. You look fresh this morning with nice clean clothes on. Where have you been?"

A. "Well, I've been taking it easy for a couple of weeks. You know the fighting on Bataan has slowed down and I've been over there seeing some of my friends, just lying around taking it easy."

Q. "How are conditions there? I've heard that food is short."

A. "No. While I was over there, some fresh bread arrived, and we threw the old bread out."

At that point we turned the radio off. Bull like that may have had some effect on the Japs, but not on us.

At the same time these radio shows were broadcasting, the message on the Army radio continued, "Help is on the way." One radio voice said, "I looked out the plane window and as far as I could see there were ships headed this way." Then all of a sudden, we received the inconceivable news that General McArthur was on his way to Australia. His words heard round the world—"I shall return"—rang hollow.

Now we were faced with orders to fight to the last man, while our General was running off to get help. What a cowardly way to treat men who knew more than anyone else what the score really was. Why couldn't he have leveled with us? He could have said, "Men, we are in a mess. Our food is about gone, ammo is getting low, and things are bad. The help from America cannot get here in time. God bless you. Do what you can." Our respect for the great General would have been preserved.

We remembered all too well the planes that were hit on the ground at Clark and Nichols Fields; the ships that sat still at Cavite Naval Base and were destroyed; and the delay in opposing the Japs when they landed at Lengayen Bay. These travesties were so needless—were so unnecessary—were so shameful. We felt like the Philippine Islands had been handed to the Japanese on a silver platter.

Even so…we continued to fight to the bitter end. On a run to our western China Sea front, a few of us were spotted by a couple of Zeroes (Japanese fighter planes) that caught us on an open road. Each truck tried to make it to a large tree for cover, but my truck was unable to get find safety. The Zeroes were so close I didn't have time to run into the jungle, so I got out and scrambled under the motor area of my vehicle as a Zero came down the road strafing. For some reason, all of a sudden he pulled up. His last bullet hit up front, so close that the dirt flew all over me under the truck. As he made his way around to come back, I took the chance to run to a rice haystack and was hit in my legs by bomb fragments. The drivers and helpers started shooting at the plane. We watched as it started to smoke and then plummeted to the ground over a small hill. One of the men went to check out the damage, and returned to say that the pilot was dead.

I was lucky. I made it to the field hospital where two of the pieces of fragments were removed. My legs were so bad that I would have to use a stick sometimes to help me push the gas pedal down. But there was no time off—I had to work.

Gerald and I knew our time was getting short and we wouldn't be able to hold out much longer. Bataan could not stand another push by the Japs. Everywhere you looked there were despondent and starving men wanting to know if we had anything to eat and asking in desperation how the front line was holding. You could read the despair and grief all over their faces and hear the hopelessness in their voices. Filipinos were walking around in a daze. When you asked them where they were going or where their unit was, they would give you this vacant look and mumble, "They all dead, Joe. No unit. All men killed."

It was true that we killed thousands of the Japs, so many that there was a lull in the fighting for several weeks. Still, they were able to bring in reinforcements, and it would start to pick up again. It was unbearable for many. Just when there was some chance of relief, hopes were dashed and our men became even more downcast and depressed. Our men grew weaker with sickness and became more disorganized, and the Filipino army was about gone. The hope of holding off the Japanese faded day by day.

Back at our company headquarters, Colonel Hurst was planning to blow up all the ammo warehouses if we were taken. On a personal level, Gerald and I had made a plan. We had stashed a small boat north of the airstrip at the end of Bataan and loaded it with supplies in the chance we could escape if we had to surrender. A man by the name of Captain Little had told us that if we were captured by the Japs, to tell them only our name and service number. He said that the Japs would expect the lower-ranking soldiers to be dumber than a higher official, so we were to say that we were privates. I remembered that advice. Also, it wouldn't be a bad idea to say we were cooks, and we were to never tell them that we were with the 75th Ordinance.

The sound of shells hitting over the west front had picked up, and at the order of Colonel Hurst, Gerald and I assisted with the demolition of the warehouse. We knew what was about to happen, and we knew that our lines would soon fall. We would also have to blow up the big ammo dump, and the job would have to be done within the next few hours.

I had only today. Yesterday was gone, and tomorrow might never come. So I took off to see Nelda one last time. It was my way of saying goodbye without actually saying those final words out loud. She did not know about the boat. Gerald and I were still planning to get away on it, but there was room enough only for two. When I met up with her, she was crying hysterically —she also knew what was ahead. She was frantically grasping for escape ideas and at one point said she would find women's clothes and dress me up as a woman in an attempt to sneak me out with the civilians.

Quietly and calmly, I had to tell her that I just couldn't do that. Finally, she gave up and simply begged me to come back someday.

When I left to go back to headquarters, she had crumbled to the ground and was still weeping uncontrollably. I had a job to do.

It was getting dark by the time I returned to headquarters. We were told that General King had signed an unconditional surrender, and that we must lay down our arms and go to one of several spots to yield to the enemy. That night we blew the top off the hill at Little Baguio. It was the biggest fireworks show ever, yet there was no celebration. After that, we were simply told to take care of ourselves and...good luck.

Gerald had one last matter he wanted to take care of. He quickly ran to our pup tent and grabbed three hand grenades, then ran up the hill to the hospital area where about nine Japs were being held. In short order, I heard three explosions and then came Gerald running back down the hill with a grin on his face. As he continued to run by me, he shouted, "Come on! They won't be eating any more of our food!"

The final mission for the heroes at Bataan was to take Old Glory down—our precious Old Glory. Slowly...carefully...quietly, we placed her in a sealed tube; and with all the respect we could show, we buried her...with every intention of coming back to retrieve her. We couldn't fathom that we would never see that flag again.

The tears flowed freely and without shame on every last face. Many—many times—more times than I can count, I thought about the men who never saw Old Glory wave again.

4

THE BATAAN DEATH MARCH

Even though we dreaded the thought of becoming a prisoner of war, Gerald and I had discussed this terrifying possibility many times, as well as various schemes we might use to avoid being captured. We eventually decided upon a plan that we thought was the most likely to succeed.

On one of our trips to Manila in February, we had found a small abandoned boat that looked fairly seaworthy, and needed only a little repair. We were elated at the thought of being able to slip away if the time came for us to do so. After checking with the people in the area to find out if there was an owner of the boat, a Filipino offered it to us. We made a few quick repairs and then stashed it in a remote area on the China Sea side of Bataan. We were confident we could escape the Japs by sea, if we had to.

Now...the inevitable humiliation had happened. General King had surrendered the troops on Bataan on April 9, 1942. And so, Gerald and I immediately put our escape plan into motion, and headed over the first hill to get to our boat. On our way, we saw soldiers destroying trucks, taking apart and throwing away guns, and wrecking everything else of value. Nothing of ours was to be left for the convenience of the Japs.

We made our way on through the jungle and noticed a clearing on the side of the mountain, indicating a road. We were high above the Maravelles airstrip and had about four miles to go, to reach the road we needed to cross, to get to where our boat had been stashed. We each were carrying a .45 caliber pistol, a BAR (Browning Automatic Rifle), and several hand grenades.

As we approached the winding road coming down the mountainside, we saw a crowd of men walking and a bus loaded with Filipinos. All of them were waving Japanese flags. We couldn't believe it! Where had they gotten those flags? Gerald was livid. "There's no way they're flying those Jap flags around," he exclaimed, and at the same time, he lifted his BAR and started firing. The bus went off the road and plunged 500 feet to the bottom of the ravine. We stood there—and just watched. For the next few moments, there was no movement and no sound. Gerald and I did not say a word to each other; we just started off again.

Suddenly, we heard a tank coming, and by the sound of it, we knew it was Japanese. Now we had a big problem. We had to get across this road to get to our boat. Having no other recourse, we decided to lay low for a little while and hope that there were no Japanese on foot. Sure enough, though, here came columns of several men following the tank going in the direction of the airstrip. We noticed that some of the soldiers were jabbing the bushes along the road with their rifles, searching for anyone who was trying to hide. Then we saw Americans and Filipinos with their hands in the air following close behind the formation.

"It's time to move back," I said to Gerald. "If they get any closer to us, we've got to get rid of these guns."

"Frazier, there ain't no way I'm throwing away my gun. If I have to, I'll shoot my way out of here," Gerald insisted. He had a .32 caliber nickel-plated pistol in his backpack that he had taken off a dead Japanese soldier. "One way or another, I'm going to get through those lines."

We had been advised not to carry anything that we had taken off a dead Jap—like guns, knives, or ammo of any kind. It was known that if the Japanese soldiers found anything on you that had belonged to one of their own, they would shoot you on the spot. I told Gerald he had *really* better get rid of that pistol in case we were caught crossing the road.

Gerald continued to ignore me and in the meantime, he sat down, pulled out a new pair of black and white shoes from his backpack, which he had bought just before leaving Manila, and put them on. He had worn them only a couple of times before.

Now there were more and more Japanese coming down the road, plus several trucks and tanks. Right in front of where we were hidden, they pulled off the road and started motioning others to also pull over. We figured they were stopping to set up camp. Our hearts were pounding so hard that we could barely hear each other as we continued to speak even lower than a whisper. Now we would have to adjust our plans—get out of the ditch we were in and go back up the hill to get across the road.

All of a sudden, we heard something behind us and turned around...six Japs were standing there with guns and bayonets pointed right at our chests. They motioned for us to climb out of the ditch and to throw down our guns. Quickly, Gerald slipped the .32 out of his back pocket and stuck it in a pocket of his backpack, then turned the backpack over. When he picked up the backpack, he knocked the gun out onto the grass without the soldiers seeing it. They continued to motion for us to go to the road and start marching. Just as I started to say something to Gerald, one of the Japs hit me in the back of my head with his rifle and shook his head back and forth.

As we walked toward the road, my thoughts went to Nelda, wondering if she was okay. I had no idea about my own future, or if I even had much of one. This was the lowest time in my life. Why hadn't the Army helped us? I was so angry that I think if a newly landed American soldier had walked up to me at that moment and offered help, I would have hit him. Here we were seized by the very enemy we had fought to keep from taking Bataan, prisoners of war facing these Japanese, for whom I had built up so much hatred. This was the worst thing that could have happened to me. I didn't know where they were taking us or what they were going to do with us. I was almost sick to my stomach with rage and despair at my helplessness to do anything to defend myself.

I wanted to take a minute to talk to God, but I felt I had no time to pray; every second, all my senses had to be totally alert of everything that was going on around me. As we walked on with our hands in the air, we met up with another group and I saw up ahead a Jap beating an American with his rifle. Another Japanese soldier, who could speak a little English, told us that we would meet with others and line up on the runway at the airstrip.

As we arrived at the runway, the Japs who had been with us moved off to the side of the road, while another group of Jap soldiers started yelling and pushing us into a large group of more Americans. We figured this was to be our shakedown. Behind us was a tank with a Jap standing up in the hatch pointing a machine gun at us, while another Jap came from behind the tank, also yelling at us. He was hitting and kicking most of the men as he ordered each one of us to line up, step back four paces, and out an arm's length from the man next to him.

We were then ordered to put our backpacks and everything in our pockets on the ground in front of us. As armed guards took their position, three Japs began to walk the line inspecting what we had placed on the ground. Each one stole anything he wanted—a watch, a ring—anything. If a man tried to move anything, he was pulled out of line and taken away. I have no clue where they took these men. There were other men who had items that they had taken off a Japanese soldier. Each of these men was led to the back of the line…and then we would hear a shot. If anyone had any guns, ammo, or knives, he was beaten or killed. And then there were those unfortunate men who had something in their pockets that a Japanese soldier simply didn't like them having—they were beaten or shot.

I was numb. I was witnessing these events, but I didn't feel like I was really there. I guess I was in shock…waiting for my turn to be executed. At the age of 17, I thought I would live forever. It was hard to come to grips with the notion this might be the end for me.

We had stood there at least an hour and a half when we were finally told to pick up our things and move down the road. Amazingly, they had not taken the candy I had in my backpack that had come with our C-rations. We had been hoarding food and other supplies for three months, saving them for our escape attempt.

No one can ever imagine how crushed and lost we felt. We were broken in spirit and were in need of food and water walking down a dusty road to nowhere—all the while suffering under the obvious malicious satisfaction of the Japs because they had defeated the Americans. Still, Gerald and I had not given up.

We started to march again, as the guards spread out, moving up and down the lines. Gerald and I continued to look for a place to take off into the woods without the guards noticing. As we went around a curve, we saw a trail leading up into the jungle…and we took it. We made our way up to a clearing; then noticed someone over on the other side. So we turned into the dense jungle and dove into some bushes, away from whoever was close by.

As we lay there very still, a couple of Japs passed by. I suppose they were looking for us. We hardly breathed. After they passed us, we started up the hill again and soon we were back on the trail. But it wasn't long before we heard something coming up behind us, and we turned to look. There were two more Japs—ready to shoot. We stopped dead, but they motioned for us to go on ahead.

As we came into a small clearing, we saw four more Japs sitting there. We could not fully understand what they were saying, but could somewhat read their motions. It seemed like the two who had caught us were explaining to the others that we had been coming up the trail.

They made us take off our backpacks and spread the contents out for their inspection. They took our watches, which oddly enough hadn't been taken at the first shakedown. They also took our candy, our shirts, and underclothes. They took everything we had left. They even took our water canteens and poured the water out on the ground. And then, to our surprise, they just told us to start walking. They didn't yell at us. They didn't hit us. They just told us to move.

One of the Japs followed us until we came to the road again and ordered us to get back into the group. He said something to the other guard, then he came over and slapped both of us. For Gerald and me, at that moment, on April 9, 1942, the Death March began.

I now had only a sun helmet, shirt, black pants, and an empty canteen hanging by a chain around my belt. Gerald wore basically the same clothes with a towel around his neck and the black and white shoes that were already hurting his feet. I figured we had already walked about 30 miles trying to get to the boat we had stashed.

In the beginning it wasn't so bad. The yelling, the constant derogatory shouting, and the beatings were to be expected. We were in a crowd with other Americans and Filipinos, and it was time to make the best of it. My dad had taught me to adjust to any circumstance as quickly as possible. This training had already saved my life several times during the fighting, but for Gerald it was not so easy. He was already complaining and worrying about everything. I had to keep telling him, "Look, we have to make the best of this because we no longer have the power to change anything. This is still a battle, and we've got to keep fighting to save our lives."

The night went as well as one could expect as we kept marching…and marching all through the night. The next morning, we saw trucks and equipment that had been destroyed by Americans lined along the side of the road. The sun was now beating down on us, and at this time of the year, it was blistering hot. As we marched out of the mountains where more Japs were gathered, the environment started to change. Some of the men were slowing down. This wasn't good. If anyone dared to stop, they were shot or bayoneted to death. My mind could not comprehend that these men were being brutally murdered in front of all of us. And there was nothing—nothing we could do.

As Japanese lined the road taking pictures, more men, who had already been sick before the march had started, were dropping by the side of the road. As we passed, a few men asked for help, but we soon found out that if we tried to show any kind of compassion, the Japs would shoot. Many men, both those who needed help and those who were willing to help, died under these despicable circumstances.

Sometimes trucks would come by with Japanese soldiers in the backs of the trucks. As they passed us marching in columns of four, they would stick their guns with fixed bayonets out between the wooden sides of the truck and try to hit the heads of those men marching in the right column. I saw several more men killed this way. Yet in spite of all these cruel and vicious murders, Gerald and I managed to stay together.

At other times, there would be Japanese resting on the left side of the road. If they saw someone who still had a ring, watch, or any other piece of value, they would take it. If the prisoner wouldn't give it willingly, he was shot or his finger was simply sliced off in order for them to take the ring.

It was the second day, and we had not stopped for any reason. We were exhausted and we seriously needed water. Most, if not all of us, were aware that there were artesian water wells along the road, so we were very hopeful of getting a drink. As we approached the first well, we could see men running in desperation to get water. We also saw two guards who were waiting. They stood there until these frantic men attempted to get just a bit of relief for their parched mouths, and then they would shoot them. There must have been at least 200 bodies around that well. Somehow water didn't seem important enough to die for, so I continued to march.

We were now approaching the first small Filipino villages where some of the gracious villagers were trying to throw us food. To make an example of them, a Jap went into the village and dragged a woman and a girl, who was about nine years old, into the road at gunpoint. The woman was pregnant. The Jap cut her throat in front of her small daughter, then violently slashed her stomach open as we passed. I saw the unborn baby hanging half out of her stomach. It was a gruesome sight and almost made me sick. The Jap then unmercifully ordered the little girl to go back to the village. When she got to the edge of the road, he shot her point-blank in the back. I had to hold Gerald back. He was ready to kill that detestable piece of garbage. He looked at me and said, "See what you did? You made me get rid of my .32 revolver, and I could have shot that Jap." I didn't say anything. Had Gerald kept that revolver, he would never have had a chance to shoot anyone.

As we marched on, we could hear men constantly screaming. Some were begging for water and food, but there was nothing you could do to help them. None of us now had anything left but the clothes on our back. The sun was blazing and the road was smoldering hot. The march and the heat were beginning to take their toll on Gerald and me as well. But we just had to survive this nightmare. We had been in so many tight spots before and had come through them. We would get through this somehow.

Now we came to a place where the Japs took several men out of line, stopping at the man marching in front of me. As I continued to move on, I saw these men being forced to shovel dirt into a bomb crater, a hole in the road that was half full of water.

As we passed close by, some of the men were so exhausted and beaten that they could no longer lift their shovels. The Japs started to kick them, and a couple of other soldiers on the bank were pushing them with long bamboo poles under the water and mud. They were being buried alive! Immediately, those of us still walking quickly changed the lines we marched in. As the marchers got a little scattered, we took our positions in the third column on the road. This gave us two men to our right and one to the outside of the road next to the ditch.

Now the men were dropping like flies. When a man fell into the road, the first truck driver of a convoy of Japanese trucks would swerve his truck to run over the body. The crunch of breaking bones made me want to throw up. The following trucks would do the same. The man would be pounded into the road like a dead dog. Would there be no end to their tortuous and inhumane treatment? The rage and hate continued to boil and flow through Gerald and me.

We saw water and were so very thirsty, but were forbidden to drink. Our bodies ached, but we were forbidden to stop. We were so very tired and weak, but were forbidden to sleep. And the march kept on. And to make matters worse, the Japs would stop along the road to drink from their canteens and eat their rations. Although my own personal feeling of hunger had somewhat lessened, it was almost impossible to bear watching them eat while we were starving. And then, there was always the unknown that could drive any sane person mad—*what terrible torture would I have to bear at any moment?* At times, the thought of death seemed like it would be a welcome relief.

By the second day, the reality of defeat had finally sunk into my mind. While I walked, it was time to take stock and think about the reality of being a prisoner of war. Never in my darkest thoughts could I have imagined the events of the past few days. The unbelievable had happened. The fight was over. The Japs had won.

I was now part of a group of defeated men marching in columns of four, on a road that I had traveled so many times with big red flags flying on the front of my truck. Only a few days ago, I, a proud American soldier, had priority over the use of this road. Everything and everyone else had to yield to me and my fellow soldiers as we drove the big trucks and furnished ammo to the front lines. Now, there were no more front lines, no more fighting for our country. Now…I was fighting for my own life.

Tokyo Rose's words had come true, and it was a very bitter pill to swallow. She was right—there had been no reinforcements. MacArthur was a liar. All his promises were empty and had proven to be just wishful thinking.

The men who fought on Bataan were like no others in the history of America. They served in honor and fought far beyond the call of duty. So many of them gave their very own lives. But for what? Now we were being subject to brutal acts by an army of barbaric Japanese Imperial troops who took sick and cruel pleasure in blatant murder, using their bayonets and sabers to slice us beaten and downtrodden men as if we were mad dogs.

As I put one foot ahead of another, I wondered why my life had not been taken during the fighting. Even if my body had been left to decay, to return to God in the same manner that I had come—ashes to ashes, dust to dust—at least a death while fighting would have been an honorable one. Now, as I looked at all the bodies along the road, I realized that here was another kind of killing field. But this time we were being slaughtered like sitting ducks, stripped of our honor and our guns—our ability to defend ourselves against such acts of horror, abuse, humiliation, and inhumane treatment. There was no one who could begin to understand what we were going through.

Then my thoughts raced back home. How lucky I was to still be alive—or was I lucky? Why was I still alive when so many others had died? Such thoughts, back and forth, would torment me at times. But at the end of all the thinking and trying to make sense of total madness, I realized that I had to figure out a way to survive this terrible ordeal if I wanted to return home. Suddenly, the will to survive came over me, and I knew I had the pure guts to make it.

The morning air moved slowly along the jungle trees, and at times the stench of death was unbearable. Yet this smell would give me some sense of satisfaction. It reminded me of the Japs I had killed. I had had my time for the past four months. Now, it just happened to be their turn…for a while. When I looked up, I could see the vultures flying around. I thought about how wonderful it would be to be one of them, to be able to just fly away or to find a few morsels to eat. It was ironic that the birds had plenty enough to eat, yet us men had no food at all. My mind would wonder at times… maybe God had thought of everything—one creature's death gives life to another. In the meantime, the Japs were definitely having their heyday. They could have been decent—they could have given soldiers who had surrendered a chance to live, but even innocent Filipinos who happened to get in their way were butchered for no reason at all. They took absolute pleasure in killing. The victory was theirs, and the loss was ours.

Once in a while I would look around to see if my friend Gerald was still there, even while knowing that if he needed help, it would be impossible to give it to him.

As I put one foot in front of another, my anger continued to grow, but I knew that for now there was nothing I could do to change what was happening. I would only end up another piece to be wasted—not given a second thought. What good would it do at this point to make an effort that would be absolutely fruitless? I knew that for now I had to accept these criminal acts. I had to do everything possible to keep my anger in check. I had to keep picking up my feet and pushing forward so I would not incur the wrath of these ruthless savages. Meanwhile, in my heart I remained proud of the times that I had not given the Japs a chance to live when I had had the upper hand.

We just had to push on as far as our bodies would take us in hopes we would make it to the finish line—wherever that was, or whenever this godforsaken march would be over. At that point I was determined that if they were going to kill me, they were going to have a hard time doing it. I was not about to give them a reason to take my life. They would have to stoop to the lowest measures to do so. I would not need a drink of water. I would not falter. I would not do anything but what I was commanded to do. I accepted my fate and adjusted quickly to the conditions at hand. With my mind made up, they could not kill me until I had exhausted every effort in my body and soul to meet whatever was ahead.

Yet there were other moments when dying wasn't such a bad idea. But…no…that would be the easy way out! I was not ready to accept that fate at this point. I had to win the battles raging in my mind. I told myself to forget about the hunger, forget about the thirst, forget about the pain, forget about the killing. Keep pushing…one step at a time. Just be numb. Don't think. Don't feel. Just move…just keep moving.

On the third day, the steps were even harder to take. More men were massacred. The bayonet killings…the beatings…I tried not to notice. At times, I started to think just like these sadistic Japanese were thinking. If I could have changed places for a while, I would have killed them all, in the same way I saw them kill Americans and Filipinos. My heart was growing hard and vengeful. Maybe…just maybe I could live to pay them back with the same treatment they had imposed on us.

As the sun rose one more time, we could see even more horrible atrocities that had been inflicted the night before. Surely, it was only a matter of time before each of us would die. Interestingly, though, the hunger and thirst were not as bad as the day before, but

I could tell that my once strong, young body was feeling the effect of this endless ordeal.

Now on the fourth day, the stench of death was even worse. The sun seemed to be even hotter, and each step was an extreme chore. My body and mind began to play tricks on me. The thought of food and water no longer worried me as much as the pain in my legs and feet. My legs were swollen, and my feet didn't feel like feet anymore. All my joints were harder to move, but I had to go forward at all costs.

I thought about what Gerald had said just a few days earlier. "We'll wait until we're out of Bataan, then we'll make a break to escape." Escape? That was impossible now. There was no one around who could help us...and our legs could not stand any attempt to run. When I glanced over at Gerald, his face showed the strain, and I'm sure he also felt a great deal of pain. During the previous night some men in our group had started singing the "Star Spangled Banner." Shortly afterwards, a machine gun burst killed at least 50 to 100.

At this point, we were moving out of the old war zone and saw a few Filipino people along the road. They tried to throw sugar cakes to us, but the guards opened fire on them. At least six of them were killed. Then the guards went into their homes, yelling and shooting everyone. Some of them ran. I saw another young defenseless Filipino woman killed with a saber.

It was the fifth day, and our ranks had severely thinned out. I began to wonder how it would feel when my eyes would no longer stay open. Would I fall asleep as I walked? Gerald and I were in the third column from the side of the road. We decided that if we could no longer manage to stay standing up, we would try to make it to a ditch. We would hide there in hopes we could get some rest throughout the day and night, and then get back in line the next morning. But for now, we were still on our feet and marching steadily forward. Gerald's new black and white shoes were agony for his feet, which were covered in blisters and open cuts. Yet, his will was like steel. If anyone could make it, he could. But in reality, how much longer could each of us really hold out?

On the night between the fifth and sixth days, it rained. Water! Was it really water? We opened our hands to catch this priceless gift. While the guards weren't looking, I turned my head up and opened my mouth to catch just a little more, while Gerald sucked a few drops from the dirty towel he had around his neck. Meanwhile, the guards continued to yell and to kill. This day was no different than any other. It was what we had to face, and we were determined to take everything dished out to us until the finish.

On the seventh night we all were so weak that picking up our feet was now out of the question. All we could do was shuffle along. There were significantly fewer of us now—sometimes there was up to 50 feet of space between the guy ahead of me and my place in line. I had lost sight of Gerald. I knew he was somewhere around me, but I no longer cared. I could hear my feet dragging, but was unable to pick them up. I no longer thought about anything except to keep myself from falling, which meant a sure death. Yet wouldn't death now be welcome? Maybe I should just drop to the ground and take a shot or a bayonet to end it all? But for some reason a flare of hope would come over me, and I knew I had to keep sliding my feet. I would not accept defeat.

Soon, even though everyone was moving slowly, the ranks started closing up again. How had we managed to catch up to the men in front of us? I looked up and could see that the Japs were directing us into a fenced-in area. Some men just stopped. Some fell down. I expected gun shots, but…there were no shots. I thought, *Oh God, please help us if this is not the end.* Soon I was jammed up tight against someone else. I thought I heard someone say, "We're going to get some rest. Let's all slide down on the ground." But there was nowhere to fall. Each body was jammed up against another body. My feet and legs were some place, but it did not seem to matter. I think I was asleep before my body touched the ground.

We were in a holding pen at San Fernando. Sometime later a blast of machine gunfire caused a rush to one side of the compound. When I looked around, I saw that the holding pen was partly empty except for some bodies that didn't move. The rush must have been an automatic reflex. I had no idea where Gerald was, but did not see his body on the ground in the morning when they ordered us to load into small railroad cars.

We were loaded one on top of another—as many as they could pack into a car. The Japs continued to beat the ones who had trouble moving. I have no idea how they decided who to beat next—everyone was barely moving.

Then they closed the doors of the railroad cars. We could scarcely breathe. The only air came from the small holes in the sides of the cars, while we sat there for a couple of hours. As the sun rose higher, the cars became stifling hot. It was a great relief when the train started to move out, and I guess we rode for about an hour. Then the train stopped, and the doors opened. I was sitting amongst many of the dead. The Japanese guards kicked and rolled their bodies out onto the ground, yelling and beating as many of us as they could, moving all of us out onto the road.

By now my tongue was swollen and hurting. I could not close my mouth. My legs and feet were numb on the outside yet experiencing deep pain on the inside. My eyesight was blurred. It was hard to remember who I was or what I was doing. I still could not pick up my feet. In the background I could hear groans and cries but did not know why. I didn't have the strength to think, let alone to see.

I just kept moving down a dirt road, one step at a time. Sometime later I could hear voices in front of me but was unable to tell what was happening. As I stumbled along knowing that my next step might be my last, someone took my arm. I thought, *Now it's my turn,* and I braced myself for the beating that was sure to come. But no, this voice was low, not loud. It was Gerald. My first thought was that both of us would be shot or bayoneted for talking. He said the march was over.

I lay on the ground. Everything was blurry. Gerald put a wet cloth over my mouth and face, telling me that I was going to be all right. At every little noise my body would jump. I have no idea how long I was there on the ground, but when I woke up later, Gerald was putting a drink of water against my lips. My mouth was so dry and my tongue so swollen. When I took a swallow, it tasted like hot water. Gerald gave me only a few small sips at a time. Later he and another person moved me to the outside of a building and sat me up against it. Men were moaning and crying all around us. Gerald and I, along with some of the others, stayed by the building until the next morning. We then went inside a broken-down barracks and fell onto grass mats on the floor. We had made it... Camp O'Donnell.

5

CAMP O'DONNELL

A few days passed. My tongue was slowly returning back to normal, and I was able to eat the one bowl of rice that was provided each day. There was only one water spigot in the camp to accommodate all the men. If you wanted water, you had to line up for about an hour before you could reach it. If you sat down while waiting your turn, a Japanese guard would come over and make you get up. I was still very weak, but Gerald had been there all along, helping me up to get water and food.

Camp O'Donnell was a Filipino army post. When we had arrived on April 15th, I had noticed that the buildings had been shabbily built, and the one in which I was to stay had a bamboo floor about two feet off the ground. I understand that some other buildings had only dirt floors. When I got to the point where I could move around, I couldn't believe the condition of some of the men. Some were dying from the toll of the brutal march; others were suffering from malaria, dengue fever, dysentery, malnutrition, scurvy, diphtheria, beriberi, ulcerated sores, and blisters.

The bamboo floors were hard—they were real hard. I had already lost about twenty pounds and had no kind of padding to lay under me. When I went outside I could see that a hospital building had been set up…if you could call it that. Actually, it was a morgue.

Those who went in never came out. It was the end of their journey. Their clothes were pulled off, and the Japanese would slide their bodies under the building until they could be buried.

I had heard that some other men from the 75th had also survived the march. One of them was Howard Leachman, from Cartersville, Georgia. He had helped me so much during the fighting while he had been in charge of the ammo going out of the warehouses. Some others from our company may have made it, too, but I was unable to look for them.

Soon the Japs were taking a few men on outside work details, if they were able to walk. Some attempted to escape while outside working, but they were caught and then shot. Some details would go out to work and when they returned, we discovered that the Japs had killed as many as five to ten of them that day. They were just left to rot by the side of the road, or maybe tossed into a ditch. Around the actual camp was a wire fence, bordered by tall grass, to prevent escape. Some Filipino soldiers did manage to get away, but it was very risky if you were in bad shape and had no one on the outside to help you make it.

During our stay at the camp, Gerald and I won some pesos in card games, but there was very little you could buy. Some men who went out on daily work details would bring back things like canned goods. We paid as much as 250 pesos for one can of corned beef. We bought only one can at a time; there was no advantage to buying extra food to save for the next day. While you slept, it would be taken. Every day at the water spigot there would be some men fighting over water and acting like animals. The language was always raw and vulgar, as it had been in the most fierce of battles. Many would lose all sense of common decency, and any type of manners or etiquette was nonexistent.

Many nights we were awakened by the noise of a Jap beating someone. Their choice of weapon was usually their rifle butts. The sounds were anguishing. After each lick there would be a scream or a moan, which eventually got weaker and weaker until you didn't hear the sufferer cry out any longer. The next morning, someone would be ordered to pick up the body and put it under the hospital building until a burial detail could get to it. When the time came to do the burial, each body would be placed on an army blanket, then each end would be tied, and a pole would be run through the knots. Two men would put the pole on their shoulders and take the body to a large shallow grave, lay it down by the side of the grave, slip the pole out, untie the blanket, and roll the body into the grave on top of many others. The whole area was constantly covered with the sickly smell of death. Dead human bodies have a very different odor from that of any other dead creatures. Once you have been exposed to it, you never forget it. It was utterly shameful, totally disheartening to see our fellow comrades treated in such a despicable manner.

Sometimes I found a place to lie down in the sun, look up at the skies, and wonder if God was noticing what was happening here. I knew He had walked along with me on the march. Even though I was still in bad shape, I was fortunate that I hadn't been shot or beaten like many of the other men. In addition, God had given me the strength to resist the desire to quench my thirst or stop to rest. Either would have been sure death.

At other times a feeling would come over me that I should just give up and go ahead and die. But every time my thoughts drifted in that direction, I would also immediately think of home and Jamie. I would begin to wonder if she had come back from her visit, and whether or not she had gotten married. I also thought about Nelda, and if she was all right. Then I would think, *I have to live to find out these answers for myself. I must live. I can't let these Japs destroy me.*

Eventually, I started to work on the burial detail, and soon we were burying two hundred men a day in camp, plus the ones killed on the work details. Each time a man would get close to death, he wanted someone to promise to talk to his family or loved ones and let them know how and where he had died. I realized that there was a strong possibility that I might die in the jungle or somewhere outside the camp, in which case my body might never be found, and I would be declared "missing in action." So, to avoid the agony that my family would endure not knowing what had happened to me, I decided to throw one of two sets of dog tags into the mass grave. I figured when someone found my dog tags in that grave, it would be assumed that my body was also part of that grave. Consequently, my family would be notified, and the message would provide some answers for them.

As the days dragged on, the death rate climbed higher and higher. We had been there only a few weeks, and I knew I could not take it much longer, so Gerald and I decided that it was best to become part of another work detail—one that left and never returned to the camp. It didn't matter which one. We knew that in time if we continued to stay at Camp O'Donnell, death would surely be our fate.

I never dreamed that a person could stand such harsh treatment as we were given at the hands of the Japs, and still live. The human body is truly a miraculous wonder. It can tolerate an unbelievable amount of mistreatment, and many times forgive the pain and abuse inflicted, and return to its original self...if given the proper time and care. But at the present time, our bodies were wasting away. Sickness was rampant. Escape was out of the question because our bodies could not stand a run for freedom. We had to just take what we were dealt, if we could stand it. We did think about maybe trying to wrestle a rifle away from a Jap. If you were successful, you could at least shoot one or two of them, before they opened fire and blew you to smithereens.

Adjusting to the constant threat of torture and death was impossible for many men. And when you gave up, you lived only a few more days. When you looked in their faces, you could see a reflection of the anguish, the oppression, and the horrors they had endured.

Soon, they were again calling for hundreds of men to go on details, so Gerald and I went out and lined up. A guard came around shoving us into different groups, and somehow Gerald and I were separated. We had been together all the way through the fighting, stood side by side in battle, and saved each other's lives countless times. At any time, we each would step up to catch a bullet to save the other. Our friendship was made of iron; it was unbreakable. It was forever. No one could say or do anything to the other without dealing with both of us.

Gerald was among the strongest and the bravest. Now, he was looking at me with tears in his eyes. My eyes were full as well. I looked across the yard and yelled, "Gerald, I *will* see you later! I *will*...." As I was pushed out the gate, I saw him standing there next to a guard, trying to convince him to let him come with my group.

It would be many years later when I would find out that Gerald had been assigned to a "bad detail" at Nichols Field and would eventually die a hero on the Hell Ship Arisan Maru. ...I owe my life to him.

The Japs loaded us onto trucks and we went to the railroad where we were transferred to flatcars. I had no idea where we were going or for what purpose, but as we traveled, I noticed that we passed by Manila and were headed south. Eventually, we were unloaded and forced to march 20 or 30 miles into a dense jungle. It was nothing like The Death March, but still, we were weaker, and marching again took its toll. This time, though, we were able to help each other without being beaten or shot.

On the way we stopped at a schoolhouse. There, three or four men were unable to go any further. I have no idea what happened to them, but they were replaced with six other Americans. Further on, we lost one more man. For all I know, his body was left by the side of the road. When we finally arrived at our destination, we found ourselves beside a river in the dense jungle somewhere in South Luzon. We were told we were there to build a road.

6

THE TAYABAS ROAD DETAIL

We finally arrived at the new camp location on May 8th, but… there were no buildings. I saw a tent that the Japanese were using as their office, set up next to the river, another tent for their guards to bunk, and a few horses. But no other buildings.

We were immediately taken to a bend in the river where there was an open space of rocks and sand…and we were told to camp there. So our group assumed we must be staying only for the night. But we found out it was our permanently assigned place to sleep. We were out in the open with only rocks and sand as a mattress. We had no materials whatsoever to use to make a camp. We were just to find a spot to lay our heads down—as if we were animals. In addition, we were told that guards would be there all night to watch us. We were placed in groups of ten and warned that if any one or two would to try to escape, the rest would be shot. We made a pact that if anyone wanted to try to escape, all ten would go or none would try.

The next morning we were awakened at daybreak by the guards. The designated cooks were already preparing some watery rice. There was nothing large enough to cook in that would hold the food for all of us, so the cooks used a couple of steel wheelbarrows.

After we ate, we had to take those same wheelbarrows out and haul dirt and wood all day in them. To get drinking water, we dug a small hole in the sand and let the water from the river fill it up. The problem was that the horses were located upstream from us and used the river to dispose of their waste, and there was little iodine left to purify the water.

Our assignment was to build a road to connect southern Luzon with northern Luzon so that the Japanese could move their troops by land rather than by water. We used picks, shovels, and jackhammers to drill the rock, and we had to break the large rocks with sledgehammers and pry bars.

During the work details, we were organized into work groups of about 20, each with a guard. The Japanese "bosses" acted like engineers who chose one American to be the head of each group, but that American had to work as well. The boss would come by and tell the head American what work he wanted accomplished for the day.

I was selected by the Japs to be the head of our group. One of the Jap guards assigned to our group was especially malicious, and we accordingly named him "Killer." On the second day, he had ruthlessly killed a man in another group. This American soldier had been so weak that he was not able to lift the sledgehammer to break a big rock, so Killer knocked the American down onto that same rock. Then Killer hit him in the back so hard that the rock crushed into his chest. He was dead within 30 minutes. The guard would not allow any of us to help him. He just lay sprawled there on that filthy wretched rock in the baking sun and bled to death.

Many men continued to get sick. Conditions were so bad the doctor at the camp could not keep up with the problems. When the doctor would tell the Japanese that a man was too sick to go to work, they would go to that man and say, "No sick—work, or get beat." Some would literally drag themselves out to work only to be beaten nearly to death. They would then lie there along the rocks and sand until we were done for the day and could drag them back them in with us when we quit work.

A couple of my close friends died at that camp. One was Howard Leachman, from the 75th. He had called me to the spot where he was lying and asked me to do something for him. He knew he didn't have long to live, and he wanted me to promise to go see his folks when I went home.

I tried to pep him up and said, "Aw, come on Howard, you're not gonna die."

"Oh, yes, I am."

There was no use to argue with him. His health had not been very good even before the Death March, and since then, he had worsened considerably. "Everyone is saying this will be over in a few months," he told me, "but I see it differently. It's going to be a long siege for us."

I then asked, "Howard, why do you want me to go see your folks? There are other men who you are closer to than me. Why don't you ask one of them?" He responded, "You're the only one here that I know who will make it home. And I know you well enough that when you promise to do something, it'll be done. I can't trust any of the others to do what I ask. So…please…promise me that you will do this for me."

"Okay…I promise."

He reached into his pocket and pulled out a tattered and threadbare billfold. He then took out a picture of his son, who had been born after Howard came to the Philippine Islands.

"This is my son. I've never seen him, but I love him. I want you to look him up when you get back and see if he is okay. If he isn't, please promise me you will find my mother and father in Cartersville, Georgia, and see to it that they take care of him." There had been problems between members of his family that had concerned Howard and caused him to think that his son was possibly being mistreated by his son's mother. He wanted his son to grow up in a Christian environment. I promised that I would do what I could.

The next few days, I would constantly check on Howard every chance I had. Each day as soon as I came in from work, I would go to him. I kept trying to encourage him. But each time he would tell me that he knew he was really close to death. It wasn't long before one of the doctor's assistants came to me as I was returning from work, told me that Leachman was close to death, and that I had better go see him.

When I got to Howard's side, he knew who I was, and said to me, "Now that you're going to do what I've asked, I can die knowing you will help my son. Please tell him I love him, and that I'm sorry I couldn't tell him myself."

I reassured him again that I would try to find his son and help him. Howard smiled at me with tears running down his cheeks. I asked three other men to pray with me, and we said a special prayer for Howard, asking God to take care of him and his son.

As I sat there beside him, I noticed that he was in excruciating pain. I could not see how anyone that sick could last much longer. Death would be a blessing for Howard. His pulse became weaker and weaker...and soon it was over for another honorable, brave soldier. I will never forget Leachman. I will never forget his love for his son. I will never forget how much he wanted to be able to live to see him. And I will never forget how much it meant to him that I would help his son when I returned to the States.

I was still on the detail where Killer was beating men every day, and almost every day we had to carry at least three or four men with us who were unable to work. Soon my day came for the beating I had watched several others get so many other times. I think Killer had wanted to beat me for some time, but I hadn't yet given him a good enough reason to do so. I had been very careful not to cross him—I knew what he was capable of doing.

We were on our way back to camp, marching four abreast. As we came to a narrow bridge across a deep ravine, Killer started yelling for us to go faster, even to run, after we had worked all day. Our pace was bound to slow down from a four-column to two men side-by-side in order to cross that narrow bridge. Since I was in charge of the Americans, I looked at Killer in the face and said, "Shut up, you blankety-blank Jap!" He looked back at me and said something threatening in Japanese, which by now I understood.

He slapped me about four times, then along came another guard. He took his rifle butt and hit me in the chest hard enough to knock me down. The guard hit me three more times, and then Killer went over to a pile of tools and picked out a pry bar about five feet long. He then told the guard to step back. I had been standing at attention, but tried to dodge the blow when the bar hit me above my left eye. I blacked out. The next thing I knew, I was in camp and the medic was putting a piece of tape across the cut, which was about three inches long.

I went in and out of consciousness for a couple of days, and I could not see out of my left eye. As soon as I could walk, though, they were trying to get me back to work. I had to buy some more time to rest and recuperate before I had to go to work again. So I would ask for help to stand up, then would fake falling and hobbling around. That act got me about six days' additional rest. For some reason, Killer didn't have much to do with me after that. Each time, I came close to him, I would stare him right in the eyes. I hoped it kept him awake at night.

My head became infected, and sometimes I could not keep my balance. When I would stumble on my way to or from work, the guards would push or slap me. When they hit my head, the impact would open the cut over my eye and make it worse. It was months before it healed.

Out of 306 men at the Tayabas Road camp, about 40 died the first month, and more and more men were becoming sick and were being beaten and starved. The American crew who usually took care of the sick men in camp were unable to take care of all of them.

There were so many getting sick that most just lay there without treatment. They either got well on their own, or else they died. When we buried someone, we simply put two stakes like a cross at the head of the shallow graves and placed the men's dog tags inside with them. It was so sad to think the graves would probably never be discovered by the Americans, even when the war was over.

The big, black mosquitoes were another problem. We were so plagued by them, that if any part of our bodies was exposed at night, it would be completely covered by these disgusting creatures. I saw men, who were so covered with these atrocious insects, it looked like they had black masks over their faces. It was hard to protect your entire body with just one blanket.

In the midst of such evil and depravity, there were occasional blessings to be found, although very rare. One such valuable treasure was a patch of bananas. My place to rest at night was at the back edge of the designated sleeping area. While I was in camp trying to recuperate from my head injury, I studied the guard and learned that during the process of making rounds, he would be away from my area from 45 minutes to an hour. While he was gone, I would pile up sand and rocks under the blanket in the shape of my body, so that it would look like I was lying there asleep.

While the guard was gone, I would then slip out into the jungle, snatch a small bunch of bananas, bring them back close to my sleeping area, and cover them up with some leaves or some brush. When they were ripe enough to eat, I would slip out, bring the bananas to my resting place, eat some of them, and then cover up a few in the sand under my blanket for later. This helped control my dysentery.

Most everyone had bad cases of dysentery. We thought if we ate charcoal, the dysentery would slow down—and there was plenty of charcoal around. So we ate it every night, sitting around with black teeth and mouths. One night, a guy just started laughing, and somebody asked what was so funny. He said, "I'll bet I've eaten a twelve-foot long, two-by-four, and all it is doing is making my crap blacker."

There were reports of lots of food around, but for many of us, that was not the case. I can remember a few times when we were given some corned beef, but it was so little that it didn't help much. In fact, it made the dysentery worse for some of the men.

One morning we heard the Japs ranting excitedly and found out that a guard had been sitting under a tree the night before where he most probably fell asleep. Two pythons had wrapped themselves around him, and by the next morning, one of the snakes had swallowed one leg and the other had his head in his mouth.

We used that incident to our advantage and told the Japanese that we had seen several big pythons in the jungle. After they heard that, they posted a guard outside their shack at night. Many times we saw large pythons in the jungle area we were clearing during the day. The Japs would get very nervous every time one was spotted or they knew one was close by. Sometimes, even if we hadn't seen a snake, we would point and say that one was out there. That would take a little pressure off us so we could slow down our work for a few minutes while they tried to find the python.

Each Jap boss was supposed to meet a daily quota by moving so much mud and rocks each day. If his crew was able to get that amount done before quitting time, he received good marks from his commander. So the bosses would promise us more rice or additional rest if we worked faster and loaded our wheelbarrows quicker.

When all the wheelbarrows were loaded, the Japs would stand out front yelling at their crews to run faster in order to beat the other crews to the dumping area. This made it very hard on those of us who were unable to keep up. Some men would fall down and then there would be the usual beating. Unfortunately, some of the healthier prisoners who benefited from this system resisted changing it.

There were other American men, working in the hospital area, who withheld medicine from the sick. Although some of us saw the Japs give medicine to the medical workers to be dispensed to the sick, it was never passed on. Instead, they told the rest of us that the Japs had refused them any medicine. At times, Americans would cause harm to other Americans. Their dishonesty and lack of integrity was disheartening. The Japanese were not always our only enemy. Even our own soldiers, frantic to survive, could turn against one another.

The situation soon reached the point where almost no one was able to work. Fortunately, the rainy season was coming, and no work could be done during that time, so we were told we would be leaving shortly.

But when it finally came time to leave, the Japs changed their minds and decided to hold us up a while longer. I had already went to the Japs and asked if we could load Turesky, a friend of mine who was dying, onto the truck. They told me he would not be going along. So I went to the doctor to ask about him. He said the Japs told him they were waiting for him to die, or they would have to shoot him. I went back to the Japs and begged them to let him go, so he would have some kind of chance to live. Still they waited, and still I begged. Finally, they had had enough. The Japs grabbed me and slapped me several times, then took me back to the area where everyone was waiting. We found out later that the doctor convinced the Japs to allow him to give Turesky some type of shot. I guess his body was just left lying there.

And so, now it was time for the rest of us to board the trucks. We had started with over 300 men, and now, after three months, there were about 25 left. We all were in horrible physical condition, so much so, that boarding the trucks was an insurmountable task for most of us. We tried to help each other, but still not all of us could get on. They may as well have asked us to move a mountain.

The Japs eventually didn't want to wait any longer, so they ordered two Filipinos to help the rest of the men climb in, and we were on our way to Bilibid Prison in Manila.

7

BILIBID PRISON, MANILA, P.I.

It is very hard to describe what we looked like upon entering the grounds of the Bilibid Prison. All of us were in terrible shape. Our clothes were colorless, filthy rags—we had not once been permitted to take a bath while working on the Tayabas Road detail. Most of the men were not able to bathe themselves anyway. In fact, most men had not washed since their capture in Bataan. Some of our clothes were wired together to keep them from falling off. Our shoes were cracked open on the sides, and the laces were gone. They were wired together as well. Our smell was putrid—the Japs would not come close to us unless it was to hit us.

The trip to the prison in Manila had been quiet. Another soldier had died along the way. As we passed through small villages, the Filipinos would take a glance at us and then quickly turn away. I saw some women put their hands over their noses and mouths and run back into their houses. The sight and smell was obviously unbearable.

When we pulled into the gate at Bilibid on August 22, 1942, a few American medics came out to take care of us, but as soon as they saw us, they immediately turned and went back inside. The Japs, likewise, came out, looked at us, and then turned around and went back inside. We just sat and waited…we were too weak to even roll off the truck. Eventually, the medics returned. They admitted that they didn't want to touch us because we were in such gross condition; and they told us we would have to find some way to get off the truck, sit on the ground, and wait. The thought and feeling of being so repulsive to others—so "un-human"—is unexplainable.

But surely someone had to do something about us. A while later, a few Filipinos came out with a fire hose and sprayed us down in an attempt to get rid of some of the filth. After this, we were told to take off our clothes. Even that was a great chore for many of us. Meanwhile, they threw us some blankets to cover ourselves. And then, there we sat while the people at the prison looked at us like we were some sort of freaks. I sure felt like one.

I already noticed that conditions were deplorable at Bilibid, although somewhat better than what we had experienced on the Tayabas Road detail. And we heard a rumor that we would soon be getting some help.

Most of the men had already contracted the usual sicknesses associated with captured prisoners. Now my body began to swell as well and my legs started to retain water, which meant I was inflicted with beriberi, the wet type. My legs swelled to three or four times their normal size, and when I pushed my thumb into my skin, I could push all the way to the bone. When I pulled my thumb out, the hole would stay there for 20 or 30 minutes. Usually, the swelling continues to move up the body, and a person's lungs will start retaining water as well. When the water moves to the victim's heart, he dies.

On the other hand, the dry beriberi dehydrates bodily fluids. I was inflicted with an unusual case—I had contracted the wet beriberi in the bottom half of my body and the dry kind on top. So I was dehydrated down to my waist. Usually, a person contracted either the wet or the dry, but not both types. My Guardian Angel was definitely with me.

Most of the men there had the wet kind of beriberi. They knew if their diet was not changed soon, it was just a matter of time before death. All you could do was try to console them.

At the prison, we were divided into groups, depending upon our illnesses and physical condition. I was guided to a building, and because I was in extremely bad shape and too weak to walk up the stairs, I was to stay in a large empty room on the ground floor. The floor was concrete where I was to sleep, and I was given nothing to use for padding under my body. At six feet tall, I had lost about 40 pounds and weighed about 135 pounds. My bones were showing through my skin, and it was not long before I developed large sores all over my body. It was agony to have to lie on such a hard floor.

I started running a high fever, and my mind would drift. Sometimes it was hard to remember my own brothers' and sisters' names. The small ration of rice I received each day was not enough to help me get well, so I had to find some way to get additional food. I realized that I must regain some semblance of health if I expected to make it out of this place alive. At times we could get close to the outside wall where we could hear people passing by. While some of us would start to tussle with each other in order to distract the guard, others would call across the wall asking the Filipinos on the outside to throw over a few things to eat, like sugar cakes. Most of the time, we were not caught trying to get food. However, if a guard from the tower did happen to see us, he would yell or shout, and then come through our area searching for what had been thrown over the wall. But by that time, we would have eaten everything, and he would find nothing.

We learned to be very resourceful and made use of anything and everything we could get our hands on that would help us to survive. In fact, we were downright experts in some situations. Many men there had a "quan," which was about the size of a one-gallon can. If you could get your hands on some scrap food, you could fix up a brew using a quan. We would set down three rocks with a little space between them, build a small fire in the yard, and cook up a brew. Whoever owned the quan can that was used to make the brew got a share of the prepared food, so owning a quan was very important and very valuable.

A guy who was seriously ill and dying had basically willed me his quan, and I would fix him part of anything I could get and share it with him until his death. Sometimes a few of us would "have dinner together." We were always looking for something to eat, and ate anything that was edible. Soon, even the few cats around were in someone's quan pot, being cooked as a stew. I also heard some managed to make a decent rat stew. The few leaves on the trees were added for flavor.

Bilibad Prison was a terrible place. A doctor mentioned to me that it was 20 times worse than during the time before the war when they had animals there, and at that time it had some of the worst conditions in the world. Even so, I got to where I could sleep on the concrete floor, but my body sores grew worse. I guess I kept my weight about the same, and slowly my beriberi did improve somewhat.

There were a few Filipinos who worked around the prison, and one day while I was on the backside of our wardroom, one of them came around to collect some trash. I started making conversation and asked him where he was from. He replied, "Alabang." That was close to where Nelda lived, so I asked him to try to find her family and tell them where I was, and that I was still alive.

About two weeks later, I saw this same Filipino motioning for me to come around the other side of a building. He had to be very careful because if the guards saw him, we would both be beaten or shot. He made sure that I saw him put a piece of paper under a rock. It wasn't until about two hours later when I was able to get back there and found that it was a note from Nelda.

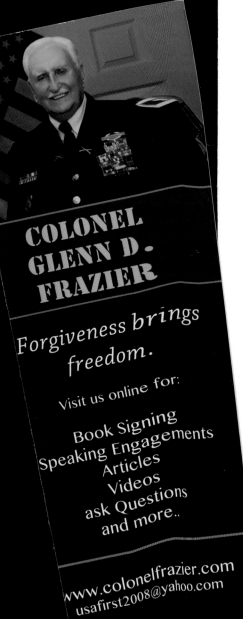
She said her family was currently involved in a guerilla battle against the Japs, and her father was one of the heads of a group operating close to Manila. She said that they would try to get some food smuggled into Bilibid, and she also told me how much she loved me.

This was wonderful news. Her family had made it out of Bataan without much trouble, except for the long walk they had to make. To avoid being raped by the Japs, she and her friend had torn their clothes and arranged their hair to look like old women. They were fortunate to get some help from other Filipinos along the way. At this point, Americans could do nothing to help them.

Holding this note, I wanted to cry and to jump for joy at the same time. I was so overcome with emotion just knowing that someone in the world knew that I was alive and cared about me. I had sort of forgotten about Jamie during that period of time, for all hope of making it back home had just about faded away. I was thinking, not *if* I would die, but *when*. After you see so many men die, there is nothing much else on your mind except to wonder when your turn will come. You try to figure which day will be the one when a Jap won't like the way you look, or when you will do something to give him an excuse to beat you to death.

Now, I was thinking about the possibility of having to stay in the Philippine Islands. That really wasn't such a bad idea. Maybe getting back with Nelda would be a good thing. But still, I couldn't help to think about going back home. Either way, hope of any kind was the only thing keeping me alive.

At one point, I got word that Nelda's brother would be throwing some oranges over the wall one at a time and for me to be ready and watch for them on a certain day. We set the time at noon for two reasons. First, the guards changed stations at that time; and second, I would know it was noontime by the ringing of the church bells nearby. We used our senses to determine all types of things to our advantage. I never did find out how Nelda's brother managed to throw the food over that high wall, but it sure was a lifesaver, and to some extent, helped my condition to improve.

It was October 1942, and at times I would wonder what it would be like to get out and return home, have a good meal, brush my teeth…read a magazine, drive my motorcycle, visit with my family, and ask my girlfriend for forgiveness for leaving—in case she had come back from her trip still not engaged, or simply wish her well if she had gotten married.

I had time to think about all that had happened to me. My thoughts would go back to the Death March, to all the men who I knew and who had lost their lives, and to all those men who I just simply lost contact with.

I would think about how God had taken care of me so far. I thought, too, about some of the Americans who were on the Tayabas Road detail who had withheld medicine from the sick, and who then died here at Bilibid. They had seemed to be in good shape when we had arrived from Tayabas. It made me think that God has His own way of handling the ones who ignore His rules. It was as though He pointed His finger at them, and then justice was served.

Near the end of my time at Bilibid, I had been talking with a Philippine prisoner who I remembered from the front lines when we set up an ammunition dump sometime in January 1942. He had been full of life and a model soldier who had fought with all his might against the advancing Japanese forces. It was so sad to now see this brave man lying there wasting away with sickness. He would tell me many times how much he wanted to go home. One day he said to me, "Frazier, I've been such a bad sinner. I'm not good enough to ask God for anything. Would you pray for me and ask Him to forgive me?" He would continue to ask me many times to pray for him.

I kept telling him that he could ask God for forgiveness himself, and I knew that God would forgive him. When my name showed up on the list to go to Japan, he begged me not to leave him. But there was nothing I could do. The day I was to leave, I went to see

him to say goodbye, only to find that he had died. How humble a man becomes when he thinks he is about to die.

There were 50 of us in the group as we lined up to move out to go to Japan. We were loaded onto a truck and were taken to the Manila docks and then reloaded onto a small freighter. As I walked up the gangplank, my spirit was crushed, my body was broken, and I was going to a land that I just knew would be the last place Americans would come if and when this terrible war came to an end.

How can a man stand tall with any self-pride when he has been defeated in battle, stripped of his dignity, weakened by starvation, beaten in slave labor camps, and disgraced by his captors? Now, unlike living in the Philippines amongst friendly faces, I was going to a land of people who despised the dirt I walked on.

Just before we left, a captain reminded me, "When you get there, you tell them you were a cook. Never say anything else, Corporal. Tell them you were a cook. If they find out you killed a Jap or had anything to do with killing anyone on Bataan, they will shoot you on the spot." Again, I remembered this advice.

As we boarded the small freighter, we were directed to go down through a freight hole and find a place on top of some lumber and other products they were delivering to Japan. A latrine was put on the side of the ship's deck for our use. Traveling with us was a fine Navy commander by the name of Callahan. I didn't know him in Bilibid, but it didn't take but a short time to get to like him.

There was also an Army captain and a first lieutenant sailing with us. The Japanese guards were not as bad as the ones we had had before, and they even let us go up on deck at times. Our ration was a small amount of rice just once a day. With this meager ration we could not gain much strength, but just holding our own was good enough, and we thanked God for that.

There were seven ships in our convoy, as well as a small gunship. Our ship had only one three-foot gun on the front deck, and Commander Callahan made it a point to find out that the gun would turn only 45 degrees to each side. He had also been the Communications Officer for the Far East and knew that submarines were somewhere in nearby waters. Right after we set sail, he met with all of us in the hold and asked what each of our responsibilities had been during the war and what training we had completed. There was a radio operator with us, and a few Navy men who had been trained as gunners on American ships.

Commander Callahan had a plan to observe the gunboat, and when it got in just the right position, he would fire the three-foot gun on deck at the gunboat. We planned to take over the radio room and overpower the guards and crew. He would then get on the radio and contact any American subs in the nearby area to call for rescue. During our cleanup details, we were also able to find out what kind of radio was aboard and where the ammunition for the guns was stored.

On various nights, one of us would ask the guard on top of the hold to allow us to use the latrine so that we could determine the location of the gunboat. In addition, Commander Callahan would stay up at night and often ask the guard for permission to go on deck. Because he was the ranking officer, the Japs sometimes permitted him to do so. At one point, when we were close to Formosa, there was a submarine alert, but no shots were fired. We all were so hopeful…but…the gun boat never came into a position where we could execute our plan.

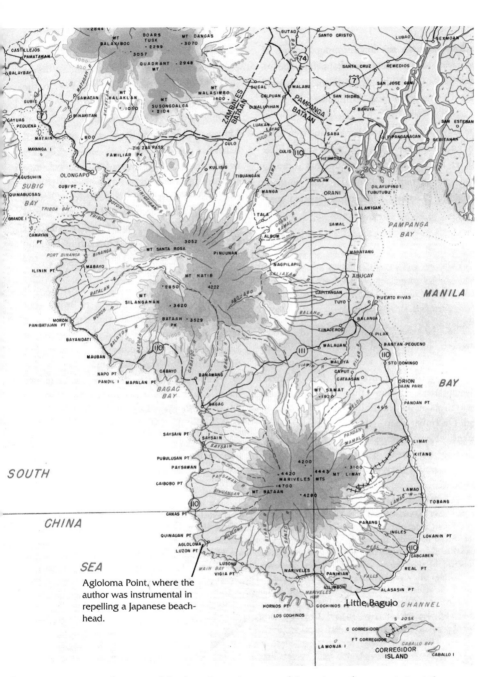

Agloloma Point, where the
author was instrumental in
repelling a Japanese beachhead.

*The Bataan peninsula, site of the heroic resistance of American forces against the
overwhelming numbers of the Japanese. Shown are the locations of Agloloma Point
and Little Baguio, site of American field headquarters on Bataan.*

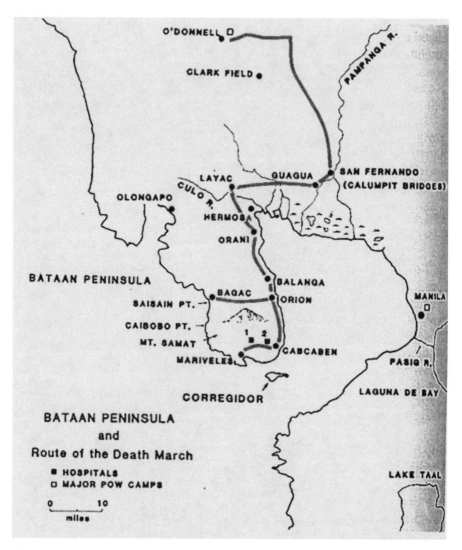

The route of the Death March. It started at Miraveles on the southern tip
of Bataan and went north and west to San Fernando. At San Fernando
the prisoners were loaded onto boxcars and taken to Camp O'Donnell.

Frazier played tackle on the Fort Deposit High School football team. His size (over six feet tall) and his physical strength probably saved his life many times over during his years as a POW.

Left: A Japanese photographer snapped this photograph during the Death March. Circled are Glenn Frazier (in front) and Gerald Block (with the towel around his neck).

Below: Prisoners sit for a rare rest along the route of the Death March. Their hands appear to be tied behind them.

Left: A burial detail at Camp O'Donnell. Bodies of dead POWs were put under the hospital building, then collected and taken to be buried. There is a body in each of the blankets.

Below: Beheadings such as this one were not uncommon. Glenn Frazier narrowly escaped this kind of death.

Left: *This drawing accurately depicts the kind of beating suffered by POWs at the whim of their guards. Only the strongest survived.*

Below: *Two POWs hours after their liberation. These men were the healthy ones.*

Sgt. Glenn Frazier after his homecoming. By this time he had regained the weight he lost in the prison camps.

Glenn Frazier in 2003. He is wearing the uniform of a colonel in the Alabama Defense Force and the Medal of Freedom awarded by the United States Senate.

8

OSAKA #1 POW CAMP

I'm not sure exactly when in October we left Manila, but I do remember it was the 2nd of November 1942 when we arrived at Moje, Japan. I had been a prisoner of war for seven months now—from the day I had been forced to join the dreadful Bataan March. And for eleven months, I had been literally fighting for my life—each and every day—since attacked by the Japanese on December 8, 1941 in the Philippines. *Was it really only a little over a year ago that I had joined the Army in Montgomery, Alabama as a 16-year-old kid?* It seemed like a lifetime ago and a world that had never been.

After we disembarked the ship and while we waited in the railroad depot, we were scorned and screamed at by the Japanese citizens, and even the little children would spit at us as we passed by. We were the captured enemy. Eventually, we were loaded onto a train—a rail car, like a livestock car with openings on the sides, in which the bitter air came through and almost froze us to death.

When we arrived at our destination, we saw a sign on a building signifying that this was Osaka, Japan, and we were then taken to Osaka #1 POW Camp. When we first laid eyes on this place, our hopes immediately rose. It looked as though there would be a building where we might get to sleep, and that there might be something to sleep on besides sand and rocks or a concrete floor. As we lined up in front of the main building, we were surrounded by many guards as well as other persons wearing regular clothing. One very ugly Japanese man was strutting around acting like he was in charge. Some of the guys couldn't help but to make a few snide comments under their breath—"Look at that ugly Jap." "Yeah…at least we had some nice-looking guards in the Philippine Islands."

Soon a Jap colonel came out with about three other people and stepped up on a two-foot stool in front of us. The ugly one stood beside him and said in English, "Let's have your attention—I'm your interpreter."

The old Jap colonel started his speech about how wonderfully we would be treated here, but warned us that if we did not obey his and all the guards' orders, we would be punished. If we attempted to escape, the escapee and nine others in our group would be shot.

Mr. Ugly used perfect English. He talked as though he was from America, and indeed, we found out later that he had attended the University of Southern California. This introductory "welcome" went on for about 30 minutes. It was the same old bull we had been told when we had first arrived at Camp O'Donnell. As the camp commander brought his speech to an end, he told us that we should consider ourselves "guests of their empire." Though we should have known better by this time than to believe anything we were told in a prison camp, still his words made us feel better.

The interpreter then told us to form into small groups and warned us again he would not tolerate anyone who did not follow orders. At this point, Commander Callahan stepped forward and gave the Japanese colonel a salute. In turn, the colonel told the interpreter to instruct Commander Callahan to bow. In reply, Commander Callahan informed him that according to the Geneva Convention, a captured officer was to salute his captor but nowhere did it say he had to bow. Our commander was then taken to the office.

In the meantime, we stood in the parade ground for 20 minutes or so, and then we were taken into the building by a guard. This would be our sleeping quarters. The floors were just dirt, and a long table had been placed in the center of the room. On each side of the table were sleeping bays, four bays high, with ladders to use to climb up into the bunks. The bunks were made of wood, upon which were laid straw mats. The mats were very little padding, but at first seemed to be better than anything we had had before. We had just enough space to lie down and room to turn over. Our shoes were to be placed on the dirt floor at the foot of our bay.

The latrine and bath area consisted of a long slit trench and two spigots to take a shower with only cold water. A chance to bathe was better than any arrangements we previously had been given. But we'd soon find out that the winters were so cold, we would always skip the baths. Even so, most of us were thinking this sure was an improvement over what we had survived in the Philippines. What wasn't different, though, was the guards. They were malicious, constantly yelling, with no let-up—screaming at us for every little matter, pushing and shoving, and hitting with their ruffle butts—over and over—there seemed to be no end. In addition to the guards who were Japanese soldiers, there were also four civilian guards who wore some type of military-style uniform. They had as much power with the old Jap colonel as anyone else in the camp.

Even with the constant abuse, I was really hoping that maybe here I would have a chance to get better…and that maybe, just maybe I would get back to the States after all. I was still in very poor health and the priority at hand was to stay alive. From the moment I landed, I made up my mind that they were not going to bury me on Japanese soil.

I wondered how Nelda was doing and also what her family had done when they found out I was no longer at Bilibid Prison. I was afraid they might have thought I had died. I did receive word later, from a sergeant in Bilibid, that Nelda's family had raided the prison looking for me. He said all of her family were able to get away, and supposedly a couple of Jap guards had been killed.

The first few days, we were given what I would call a good-sized bowl of rice in the morning and also a rice ball and a bread bun for lunch. Then at night, we received a little more rice than was in our breakfast bowl. Each day we were up at 5:30, got dressed, and were taken to the parade ground for our morning exercise. Our old clothes had been taken away and we were given Japanese soldier uniforms to wear—used—of course, and already filled with body lice eggs. It didn't take long to discover that you were never alone with them crawling up and down your body day and night.

It was really cold in Japan, and the uniforms just weren't enough to keep us warm. We never…never felt warm. Our barracks had no heat whatsoever, so we bundled up together at night, wearing our clothes in an attempt to stay halfway warm. The guards were unmerciful and would come into our barracks a few times at night and force us to get back to our own bays. As soon as they would leave…we would pile up again. But even with all of us stacked up like a pile of pigs, we still were cold. And unfortunately, someone usually had to go to the latrine every five minutes, so our sleep was limited at best.

After surviving Camp O'Donnell and the Tayabas Road detail, I had no friends left. Now, it was up to me to make some new friends, and it didn't take long to find some good men. It was easier to find someone you could trust when everyone had already been prisoners of war for as long as we had. We each were given a POW number. Mine was #632. Our pictures were taken, and we were divided into groups of ten. We had to buck up and just try to make it day by day.

Gradually, we became more familiar with Japanese words that were used regularly by the Japanese soldiers, which made it easier to understand them. "Old Ugly" certainly understood every word we said. At first we thought maybe he would be somewhat decent towards us, but he turned out to be just the opposite. He would make sure the guards beat us for any little so-called infraction. Sometimes, when Old Ugly would turn to walk away, someone would say, "Just wait until the USA wins this war, then we will kick your butt." He would turn around abruptly and scan the group to try to determine who had spoken, but no one would tell him. There was no one in the camp who did not hate him.

Our work details went out each morning about 6:30, and came in about dark. The work involved unloading ships, loading and unloading railroad cars, and working in lumberyards, foundries, and factories. It was tough, back-breaking labor. And along with the work always came the beatings. The Japs hated us. Sometimes the bosses at the worksite took the liberty to stand us out in the open and beat us for no reason at all. They just wanted to beat an American. The guards would stand by and did nothing to stop them.

We did have ways of getting even, though. Our main objective was to destroy anything we could "accidentally on purpose." This gave us a goal and a purpose for living. We weren't able to serve our country on the front lines or engage in regular battle, but we could certainly stay in the fight by sabotaging any Japanese efforts to build weapons and increase supplies.

After just one week at Osaka, they stopped serving us our noon bun, and even though we were told we would get more rice, they didn't follow through. Commander Callahan informed us that we were not going to work and would go on strike until we got our buns back. He told us he would report to the camp commander's office and simply tell him, "No buns, no work." He furthered ordered us not to move or go anywhere until he told us to do so. If we disobeyed his order, he would deal with us as hard as the Japs had.

We just knew he would be beaten badly and that all of us would get the same. But it wasn't long before he came back and said our rice would be increased at each meal. Huh? We won? … We won. How had he accomplished that? Little did we know, though, that our rice from then on would be served with worms. At first we covered up the little white creatures with their beady black eyes looking at us; soon, though, we would just eat them as though they were added meat.

As the winter wore into February 1942, the air became like ice. The north wind would blow right through our Japanese clothes. Most of us stuffed cement bag paper inside the uniforms next to our body, and it actually helped. Not surprisingly, many of us became sick. I got double pneumonia and lay in what was the sick bay area for three weeks with a high fever, sweating, and then freezing, and then sweating again. I was so sick I didn't realize how bad off I was. Commander Callahan did manage to get me some oranges but could not find anything that would break the fever. It's a wonder I made it.

Even while I was still so weak, sick, and hungry, I was forced to go back to work. And of course, I was beaten time and time again because I just couldn't do as much as they yelled at me to do. There were always harsh blows by the rifle butts. The Japs also liked to dip their bare hands into cold water and slap our tired faces at an angle that made our faces swell on contact. Still, this was nothing compared to what I was yet to experience.

I was marching with some other prisoners through the streets of Osaka, returning from a day's work. It was bitterly cold and my hands were lifeless and numb, so I placed them into the pockets of my ragged pants trying to find just a little protection. As I entered the camp gates, I noticed a Japanese guard pointing his finger at me, calling me to the attention of another guard. Later, in formation along with the other American POWs, I again noticed the same guard pointing at me and walking in my direction. Then he instructed me to follow him. I really didn't think much about this at first, and I had no idea what to expect. I followed the guard into the camp commander's office with the interpreter walking beside me. I was ordered to come to attention and bow to the major, who was sitting at his desk. A few moments later, the interpreter came over to me and said, "You were marching down the road with hands in pockets, and that is not permitted for Japanese soldiers!"

I replied, "I'm not a Japanese soldier. I'm a prisoner of war!"

After hearing the major shout in Japanese to the interpreter, I was told in English by the interpreter, "The same rules apply to all POWs!"

"I didn't know that," I answered. In a faint voice I sincerely asked the interpreter, "Why don't they tell us their rules?" To myself I thought, *If I knew all the rules, I wouldn't break them.*

The major screamed at the interpreter, who translated: "You are an American soldier and you do not march with hands in pockets!"

I responded bluntly, "Let me know the regulations, and I will obey."

The interpreter again translated my answer for the major. With a shocked look on his face, the major jumped out of his chair and whacked his clenched fist on top of the desk. I knew now that I had really provoked him. By the manner in which he spoke to the translator, I could tell he was furious with my reply. He arose again quickly from his seat and walked toward me, and the guard made me bow once more.

The interpreter said, "The commander does not like your attitude!" At that point, the major pulled his sword out and nicked my throat. I felt the blood streaming down my neck.

"Prisoners can be executed for disobeying orders!" the interpreter continued. All I could do was stand still as thoughts of terror ran through my mind. I stared into the major's hateful eyes. I never took my eyes off him, not for a moment.

All of this…*for just walking with my hands in my pockets.* A strange feeling came over me, and I suddenly knew this was a very serious matter. The major yelled at the guard and the interpreter said, "Take him outside! The major does not want blood all over his floor!" I began walking out of the office, with the rifle point of the guard behind me pressing into my back. He then ordered me to stop. I came to a complete halt, as instructed. I stood there waiting at attention for the next command, when I began thinking of and seeing myself buried in Japanese soil. My mind raced and I felt an immense fear, yet still, somehow, I felt I had a fighting chance.

I heard the commander and interpreter coming out and standing adjacent to where I was standing. As they were speaking back and forth in Japanese, the only thing I could do was stand still. I was then ordered by the guard to bow one more time to the major. And I complied.

"The major is going to execute you, so all the men will know that breaking regulations won't be tolerated!" the interpreter announced. The major walked in front of me and pulled his sword out again and put it to my throat. They expected me to beg for mercy, and the interpreter asked, "Do you have anything to say?"

"I guess I do," I told the interpreter, as I looked into the major's eyes. And then these words came to me, and to this day I have no idea where they came from. *"He can kill me,"* I replied, *"but he will not kill my spirit. And my spirit will lodge inside him and haunt him for the rest of his life."*

I was asked by the translator to repeat what I had uttered. A terrifying feeling came over me instantly, and my blood flushed over my entire body, making me absolutely burn with horror.

I said, still staring into the major's eyes, *"He can kill me, but he will not kill my spirit. And my spirit will lodge in his flesh for his entire life! The Americans are coming, and any Japanese who kills an American without just cause will have their spirit haunt them forever!"*

I did not grasp at first what I had actually said, and I was prepared to dodge the sword if the major made a move to swing it at me. I watched his every move, never taking my eyes off him. All of a sudden, a mysterious expression appeared on the major's face. Then, to my amazement, the major took three steps back and lowered his sword. I gazed up to the sky and said, "Thank You, Lord." This was the first time—the only time—I had seen a Japanese soldier back off from an execution.

The major then ordered the guard to take me to the pit—the dark, black hole in the earth that was used for solitary confinement. The guard, with his weapon shoved into my back, thrust me towards the hole—a five-foot, by five-foot, by five-foot hole in the ground. As the Japanese guard lifted the cover to the opening, I wasn't sure that I had yet survived this ordeal. He motioned for me to get down inside. Looking down into the depths of that dark abyss, I started to try to get my six-foot frame in. Then from an abrupt shove or kick by the guard, I landed head first, face down. My face and neck were slammed into the dirt. Then…I wiped the tears from my eyes.

The cover to the hole was shut and bolted down. It became pitch black. If I had not yet already been through hell, this was surely it. My body started shaking all over as I tried to get comfortable in such a cold, cramped place. Soon, the truth of what had just happened settled in my bewildered and hopeless mind. Everything had happened so fast, but I was still alive. And yet, I was sick to death with fear that they would come back at any moment to finish the job.

Later I would be told that I lay there in utter blackness for seven days in my own body waste…hot…exhausted…frail. When I had first been tossed into the hole that evening, I had not been given any food or water since early that morning. Later, a small scrap of rice ball was thrown into the hole from time to time, and I had to squint my eyes from the light of the sun when the cover was unlocked and raised. I remember that there was a half-filled bottle of water thrown down at me at some point, and I kept it close to me at all times, sipping it cautiously. I couldn't keep track of time, and often, I had no idea if it was day or night. Each time I heard a sound, I wondered if someone was coming to execute me, and at times, dying seemed to be effortless compared to the torment that I was now going through. *When will this agony end? How much longer will I have to suffer? Oh, God, just take me....*

Alone...so alone...pitch-blackness...so cramped... hungry... so much pain.... My mind started to played tricks on me. At times I would think of home and my family back in Alabama. At other times, they seemed so far away. *Do I even have a family? Do I have brothers or sisters? I can't remember their names. Where am I...?*

Then...without warning...the cover was opened, and I thought, *Is this the end? This has to be the end..."* And from the depth of my soul, I prayed it was. As the bright sunlight filled the entire hole, I saw the outline of a body. His silhouette looked dim. I was totally dehydrated and was so close to death. I couldn't feel, and even though I wanted so desperately to, I wasn't able to stand to my feet. Each time I tried, I became extremely dizzy and nauseated. Finally, after several attempts, I was able to get one hand placed on top of the outside of the rim of the hole. A guard stomped on my hand and screamed at me, "Get out!" My legs wouldn't stop shaking. It was just so hard...I kept trying and kept falling. As I placed my second hand on the rim of the dirt hole, the guard finally had had enough and yanked on both of my hands, dragging my lifeless and weakened body out onto the ground. He kept kicking my side with his booted foot as I lay there semi-conscious. As he continued to kick even more, I felt my body roll over with my back on the dirt. Still shouting at me, he gave me a lick on the head with his rifle butt, and I fainted.

I have no idea how long I lay there unconscious. I could see the barracks in the background when my vision started returning. I wanted so desperately to get there, but I just simply couldn't rise to my feet. As I started to barely crawl on my hands and knees, I heard footsteps coming from behind me. He kept screaming. I wanted to go faster, but couldn't. The continuous screams...the constant blows from the rifle butt...slamming against my hips, legs, and back. My body moved with each powerful blow. I just wanted to reach the barracks where I hoped one of my fellow POWs would surely help me.

Again my sight grew dim. Through the grueling pain, somehow I gained enough strength to start crawling once more. I was almost to the point where I was going to ask the guard to shoot me. I have no idea how long I had been crawling toward the barracks when I finally felt someone pulling me along. Could it really be that I had made it? With agonizing relief, I was given a drink of water. How absolute precious it was to have someone place a few drops of water in my mouth when I was one breath away from death.

As I lay for days in the sick bay, I thought constantly about getting back to work. And I thought again and again how important, how very serious, it was that I maintain control over my anger. It was a life-and-death matter! From now on, I had to keep control over what I said and how I reacted. Was it really only a short time ago that I was a kid who had lost his temper in a bar in Montgomery? Where I had wrecked the place with my bike, simply because I didn't want to leave when told to and was determined to finish drinking my Coke? How petty—how unimportant that seemed in comparison to the horror I had just lived through. I had gone through hell and survived.

I realized how close to death I was, and if I wanted to ever return to the USA, I had to gain control over what I said and did. I decided not to get that mad ever again. I would just get even.

In spite of this horrifying experience, there were still always trials that were difficult to handle and it was almost impossible to hold back from reciprocating and lashing out. As we trudged down the streets, little kids would run out shouting and cursing us, kicking and spitting on us. We were scum. They had been told that we were American cowards, dishonored by our country, and that we were unable ever to go back to America.

As time went on, we discovered life was not any better here at Osaka. Our lives were threatened every day and night. The guards would change every two weeks, and the new ones who had fought on the front lines were very bitter and determined to get even and make us Americans pay.

A particular favorite way to inflict pain was to make us stand at attention while holding a large piece of iron over our heads as long as possible. When we could no longer hold it up and dropped the iron, they would give us a severe beating.

By now we had learned some unobvious ways to defend ourselves, like growing a beard to protect our faces. We also discovered that when we suffered through a beating, it was an absolute must to always look the Jap straight in the eyes. If we looked to one side or the other, they would try to knock our heads off.

Unfortunately, here again, there were some Americans who tried to make friends with the Japs in order to protect themselves and alleviate their own suffering. They felt it necessary to report details about other prisoners which provoked the Japs to beat other men nearly to death. Accordingly, we formed a group to take care of those selfish type.

Because we were always hungry and never had enough food, we became real thieves. We would steal anything edible we could find in the factories where we worked. The real prize was to come upon a carelessly placed Jap lunch box. To chow down on a respectable plate of rice and fish was worth a good beating.

Almost every man had a six-inch hollow bamboo cane with a point on one end. We called them our "bird callers." While unloading rice in bags made of straw from ships or railroad cars, we would back up to a stack of those rice sacks as though we were resting for a few minutes. We would stab the pointed end of the sticks between the straw of the sack and into the bag. Then we would bump the sack with our elbow, and the rice or beans would flow into our pockets. If the Japs came toward us, all we had to do was pull our bird caller out of the rice sack, hit the bag with our elbow, and the sack would close. You couldn't tell that it had been touched. When on this type of detail, we could manage a whole mouthful of raw beans or rice at times. We all became the best thieves in Japan. In fact, we could steal while they were looking straight at us.

We *always* needed more food. When we went on details where there was nothing to steal to eat, we put another plan into action. We would rotate the "fainting trick." Someone would faint each day, and the rest of us would have to carry the "sick" man on a litter back to the camp, where we could find something to eat. This plan worked…but just for a while.

There was a guy in our group who didn't have the guts to faint because it also meant you would have to endure a beating by the guards on the detail or when you got back to camp. When the day came for his turn to faint, the coward couldn't bring himself to do it…not even for the sake of the rest of us. So, a guy from Chicago, who weighed about 180 pounds, took it upon himself to fill in for him. Soon we heard a big commotion out behind a large stack of lumber. There was our hefty friend laid out, faking a faint. As relatively healthy as he was, it became pretty clear that not only was he faking, but all our fainting had been an act as well. So we all were lined up, slapped and kicked, after which we had to lug that big guy several miles back to our quarters on a stretcher. It was not an easy job.

Under the bitterly cold conditions, nearly all of us were sick to some degree, and a few were always very dangerously ill. We had no one to rely on but ourselves, and again we came up with various ways to help ourselves get better.

One of the best techniques was a kind of laying on of hands that I called acupressure. I don't remember who first had the idea, but it may have been a Blackfoot Indian from Minnesota. When someone desperately needed help, one of us would cup our hand and place it over the navel of the ailing man. We would hold our hand there for about 30 minutes. After a while our hand would grow hotter and hotter as would the belly of the sick man. We often found this technique to be amazingly effective, and sometimes the prisoner who had been sick would be up and around the next day! It's amazing how comforting the gentle physical touch of another kind human being can be. Because we slept so close together, it was always easy to reach over and help the man next to you.

There would be times when a detail would have to travel a longer distance to work. We were often taken on these trips by a Jap driver we called Barney Oldfield, after the old race car driver. He drove that old charcoal burner truck as fast as it would go. The brakes were not so good, and many times he had to drive off the road to keep from hitting a car or bicycle or buggy.

One day he showed up with a stake-body truck that used gasoline. There was room for about 25 POWs. We all climbed aboard, and Barney started down a long, straight road alongside a train loaded with Japanese citizens. It wasn't long before the people on the train started to yell at Barney, while the train engineer blew his whistle. Barney then blew his horn, and the race was on! We guys in the back soon realized this was not going to be your typical joy ride. This was serious, and we wanted no parts of it. We started yelling for him to slow down, but he was enjoying himself too much.

The faster we went, the more excited the people on the train became. We were scared, especially when we realized that our road had to cross the railroad tracks ahead. At the speed we were traveling, there was sure to be a great collision if the train didn't slow down or if Barney didn't stop. Now, most of us were standing, and we were really yelling! There was no way at this speed we were going to make it alive!

But Barney kept going…and kept going fast. Just as he got to the crossing, the train blew its whistle again. Barney crossed the tracks…and our truck was hit in the right rear corner of the stake body. The impact from the train slung the right side of the truck into the ditch. The train kept going.

Barney gassed the truck out of the ditch and then pulled over for all of us to get off—at which time we all had to excuse ourselves! Lucky enough, only one of us had fallen off the truck and was hurt.

In the POW camp there were also about 35 East Indians who we referred to as the Hindus. They had been seamen on British ships that had been sunk, and had been fished out of the water and brought to Japan. These Indians had the right idea. The Japs could not make the Indians understand any orders…because the Indians pretended not to understand. Even a Jap who could speak English could not get them to comply. The Indians could speak English as well, but would never speak it in front of a Jap interpreter.

Sometimes we would see them across the fence from us working on a detail, and the Japs would start to beat one of them. In that situation, the entire group would get in the middle talking that Hindi language, and it was like a free-for-all fight. Even so, the Japs didn't treat them like they treated the Americans. If it had been us trying to pull a stunt like that, they would have started shooting. Many times, the Japs had a hard time getting the Hindus to work, and it became a downright circus. It would take two or three Hindus to carry one ten-foot long, two-by-four. The Japs would yell, "Hi yaka!" which meant "Hurry!" At this, the Hindus would stop, put down the two-by-fours, and send one man over to the Jap asking what "Hi yaka" was all about! It was amazing.

One day, the truck the Hindus were riding in was hit by another truck. All of them were hurt to some degree, and when they arrived in camp, you never heard such a racket as them complaining in Hindi. No one could understand all of them talking at once! Every morning in the cold of winter they would get up, go to the shower spigots, and take a bath in that cold, cold water. They explained that they were washing away all the evil spirits for the day. We

Americans were so cold we could not take a shower at any time, but somehow these Hindus managed it.

The British were another group of POWs who were separated from us by a fence and imprisoned in the back of Camp #1. They had been there long before we Americans had arrived. We did not realize that for a while they had been getting our portion of rice, cooking and eating it. We had noticed that they looked in pretty good shape, so we kept an eye on them through the fence to see what was up and how much rice they were getting at each meal. It didn't take long to figure out that they were getting twice as much as we were.

We talked this situation over with our Commander Callahan, and he took it up with the old Jap colonel, only to be told that we were already getting enough rice. So we then talked Old Ugly into getting us permission to visit our British friends.

There came a day when we did not have to work, and we were allowed to go over and meet our neighbors. There were about 350 of them and only 75 of us. As the gates opened, we Americans rushed in with blood in our eyes. Instead of passing out handshakes, we fanned out and were able to kick or hit just about everyone there.

They were running all around and begging us not to touch them. Soon the sergeant major came forward asking why we wanted to fight his men. We told him about the mangy ration we were getting and demanded our fair share. The sergeant major agreed he would fix the ration problem, and sure enough we got more rice.

Osaka #1 was also used to house merchant seamen whose ships had been sunk by German raiders on the high seas. The sailors who survived the sinking were fished from the water by the Germans and somehow found their way to Osaka #1. They told stories of the Germans machine-gunning many of them in the water before others were picked up. We had just about every nationality at Osaka, and everyone had their stories to tell.

Even though we couldn't trust every American prisoner, those of us who wanted to get some type of revenge against the Japanese were able to find each other. On one occasion, a Jap was up on a ladder in a foundry trying to fix an electric crane. As a POW ran by the switch close to the door, he flipped it on. The charge knocked the electrician off the ladder and sent him to the hospital.

At another time, we developed a plan that probably had no chance of succeeding, but one we were hoping we could get away with. It was another "accidentally on purpose" scheme. It was understood that if one of us was to replace a Japanese worker so he could be sent off to the Army, we would do such a shoddy job that it would prevent them from sending that person off.

We felt it our duty to disrupt their war effort in any way possible. This also meant destroying anything or stealing anything of value that would slow down or stop production.

Once we were unloading machines from freight cars. The Japs told us that the equipment had come from Britain and that parts were not available to them, so the handles must be protected. This was a *good* project for us. We intended to get to this machinery before it left the yard and break every handle on every one of them. To hide the damage we loaded the equipment with the fronts to the truck's side body so the Japs could not see the handles. Before the trucks left the yard, every last handle had been broken or thrown away.

If they left a truck unattended with the hood up, we would do our best to fill the oil supply with as much sand as we had time to pour in. Many times we would unload wooden barrels of liquid, and if it was about quitting time, we would make some kind of hole in the bottom of a barrel. By the next morning, no matter what it was, the liquid would have leaked out. Sometimes, though, depending upon what it was, the liquid would not have soaked into the ground, and we would be questioned about the incident. We concocted all kinds of answers for the guards. If a Jap or Korean worked the day before, but was not there when the damage was found, we would put the blame on him. Sometimes we would get beaten anyway.

Sometimes it was necessary to start a fight among ourselves to draw attention away from the culprits. We distracted the guards anyway we could.

One day, the guards pulled us out into the parade ground for what they called "drills." Old Ugly, the translator, reminded us—once again—that we were never going back to America and that we needed to start learning more Japanese, as well as how to march correctly, and obey drill orders. It turned out to be a total flop! We were about like the Hindus. The Japs thought we were going to learn "the goose step"—quickly lifting our knees high against our chests then slamming our feet down against the ground. They also wanted us to speed up our steps. None of us were in any shape to do that.

During this "training," before I thought about what I was doing, I had slid my feet without picking them up at all. A Jap with his fixed bayonet came running toward me and hurled his bayonet into my knee, slicing a gash about two inches long. The tip of the blade went all the way to the bone, and I was unable to move my leg. As I rolled on the ground in agonizing pain, I felt his boot slamming me in the back. The guard forced me to lie there until the drill was over, then had two other POWs drag me by the arms back to the barracks.

Commander Callahan came out demanding that they let the POWs bring me to the sick bay area. It took about four weeks before I could walk on that leg. I realized again that without working, I would slowly drift into permanently being unable to get around. The next step after that would be death. So hip-hopping or whatever I had to do, I did it in order to get out of there. The wound even turned blue, but I wasn't about to tell the American doctor until much later.

Sometimes, on our way to work, we would often see a Jap soldier walking down the street with an American Red Cross box under his arm. At that time we had never received anything from the Red Cross. I would ask myself, *Why is our country sending boxes for us, but not making sure that we receive them, and instead permitting the Japs to eat the contents?*

Later, I received one box from home. Even though my family had no idea where I was or if I was alive or dead, they had put a box together and mailed it through the Red Cross. Somehow, the box made its way to Osaka #1 POW Camp! What a wonderful thrill! It contained a picture of my mother, dad, one of my sisters, and a couple cousins. A letter was inside that was marked all over by the Japs, but even so, it was still from home. This brought back so many memories. I savored the one chocolate Hershey bar, but after I swallowed the last bite, my face was flush and my body felt like it was on fire. What a reaction to a five-cent candy bar!

Another small but very valuable blessing was a hat I was able to make for myself. When I was eleven years old, my leg had been cut with an axe at school, and I had to stay in bed for two weeks. During my time at home, my mother had showed me how to crochet a rug. Well, I put that knowledge to use and with an old pair of wool pants, I was able to cut them up and make a crude-looking helmet with earflaps coming down over my ears. Some of the guys told me they wanted that hat if I died. As we walked through the streets of Osaka, the people would laugh at my helmet, but it sure kept my head warm. It was the only part of my body that was warm.

Osaka was also where I learned the koolie trot. Sometimes we were ordered to use a Yaho pole to carry any variety of items, and you definitely needed to know how to do the koolie trot if it was a liquid you were carrying. A Yaho pole was a stick about six feet long that you put over your shoulders. It had a rope at each end about two or three feet long with buckets tied to each end of the ropes. You would hold one rope in front of you with your right hand and with your left hand hold the other rope. That would help, but when you walked, the two buckets would start a backward and forward motion that would splash the liquid all over you.

It was a very perilous situation when the liquid you were carrying came from the bingo, that is, the slit trench. Using the Yaho pole and buckets was our only way to carry away the waste, so learning the koolie trot was a must. You took very small, fast steps forward, and no quick stops. If you didn't follow these procedures precisely, you would be covered all over with a disgusting odor on top of the bad smell you already had from not taking a bath for six months.

It was now close to the end of our first year in Japan. The winter of 1942-1943 had been a rough one. Scarce food, light clothing—we froze all winter. If a person cut or hurt his hand, it would not even bleed. And now my teeth were giving me problems.

When I had joined the Army, I had had a perfect set of teeth. Now one of my back wisdom teeth had to be pulled. So I was taken to a "dentist." When I walked up to his "dental chair," I noticed that all the tools laid out on a glass top table had water circles around them.

The "doctor" was a very small man, and his chair was close to the floor. He did not give me anything to deaden my gums. He simply took a knife, opened my mouth, and began to cut all around the bad tooth. Then he stuck some kind of packing in my mouth and let me sit for a while. When he returned, he had some type of pliers in his hands. It made me think of how my dad would pull our old mule's teeth on the farm.

He started to tug hard on my tooth with all his might, but could not get it out. So he put one foot on the chair armrest and the other foot on the seat beside me. When he pushed down, the pliers went against my lower jaw. When he pushed down again, the tooth came out, and along with it came my jaw out of its socket. Pain! Intense pain! When I asked him what he was going to do about my jaw, he said the American doctor could fix it back at camp.

When I returned, Commander Callahan went to see the old colonel to complain about this type of treatment. Eventually, we were able to work my jaw back into place.

At other times, some of us were used as experiments while in sick bay. I guess they figured we were going to die anyway. We were never told what the purpose was for the experiment or what effect it would have on us.

Eventually, Commander Callahan told us that they were going to pull him and send him to a camp where they imprisoned officers. That was bad news for us—he had proven that he was an all-American officer. We hoped his transfer would be for his benefit. As the ranking officer in our group, he made sure that everyone was treated the same, no matter what rank. At one time on the ship ride coming to Japan, a captain had tried to buck the chow line. Commander Callahan went to him and tapped him on the shoulder. "Hey, to the back of the line, like everyone else. Let me remind you that we are all POWs now." Time and time again, he stood up to the Japs, always taking a great risk, for the benefit of us all...and never complained once to my knowledge. That was more than you could say about other officers. The Commander saved my life...more than once.

During my imprisonment at Osaka #1, I was able to make only a few close friends. I had been sick so often—my bout with pneumonia, solitary confinement in the ground, the bayonet wound, the extraction of my tooth, and there was always the beatings. During the time I was alone, it was hard not to think about what the Japs were saying. *You're never going to return to the USA. Your government doesn't want you back. You need to learn Japanese...you need to learn our ways...you will remain here for the rest of your days....*

Yet my thoughts were more about going back home than ever. Nothing they said convinced me that the U.S. government would not allow us to return home. I might have believed them in weak moments, but after receiving the Red Cross box from home, it was amazing how much strength and hope that small delivery built up in me.

Through all the beatings, starvation, and torture, even when they jammed sizzling hot wire beneath my toenails, I was not about to break...even when they threatened the firing squad. Whatever it took to survive—stealing food, dragging myself around in pain, ignoring the mental persecution—I was determined that I would survive, that I would behave and stay out of their way. I was determined that I would do nothing that might cause them to single me out again, but still, I would take every opportunity to destroy anything that could delay or disrupt their efforts in the fight against our country.

In the meantime, it would have been so wonderful to know what was happening in the world. Sometimes we would get hold of a newspaper that showed the location of a sea battle close to Japan, and this would give us some hope. Otherwise, we were never given any information about how the war was proceeding...except that it was lasting much longer than most expected. I would often think what Howard Leachman had said to me as he was in dying at the Tayabas Road detail. "Everyone is saying this will be over in a few months, but I see it differently. It's going to be a long siege...."

9

TANAGAWA

Sometime in the middle of 1943, the Japs moved all the Americans out of the Osaka #1 Camp across the bay to a village by the name of Tanagawa. Our living quarters were of the same design as those that we had in the Osaka #1 Camp. On the same day that we arrived at the new camp, 225 Americans also came in from the Umeda Bucho Camp. In all, there were 335 of us. The next morning, every one of us was taken to the same job site. It appeared that they were building three very large dry docks on the side of a hill. From the look of it, they had been working on the project for some time.

As we lined up, we were organized into groups and assigned a Jap *honcho*. Some of the guards who had been at Osaka came along with us, as did some of the guards from Umeda Bucho. It wasn't long before we quickly dubbed them with our own particular titles according to their appearance and demeanor—the project boss was Hitler, and Mussolini was a group boss. Another of the guards we called Sir Baloney Bird.

It turned out that these dry docks were to be used for large ship repair. The walls were being covered with granite rocks polished like diamonds to a beautiful finish. We first watched as a few husky Koreans, with racks on their backs, would load one rock into the rack, carry it up the walkways and ladders, and then drop it in location for the next cement run that would hold the rock in place. The Koreans could carry only one piece of granite at a time because of its weight and size. We Americans, in our weak condition, could never carry even one.

There was a large cement mixer that was being used to mix all the cement for the project. The cement, as well as other supplies, was then carried on small cars that ran on narrow gauge railroad tracks which extended throughout the job site. These cars were also used to carry dirt and rocks. At the one end of the tracks on the dry dock, the excavated dirt and rock were loaded onto the cars. There was a winch at the top, and a cable would be hooked to the last car. The winch operator would lower eight or ten cars at a time for loading, and the flagman at the top would tell the winch operator when to pull up the cars. The POWs would then push the cars (two men per car) around the track to a boat ramp that extended out over the water where a barge would come alongside the ramp. The rocks and dirt would then be dumped onto the barge and then be carried out and dumped into the bay. We were assigned to other jobs as well, but this was our main function while working at the docks.

On one side of the prison camp there were convicted felons—inmates who had been already doing most of the work on the project before we had arrived. On another project, the Japanese were building small submarines, a few of which were visible. When the Japanese workers accomplished a certain amount of work, they would knock out the blocks under the keel, slide the small submarine into the water, and finish it as it floated. Then they would tow it away for final fitting out.

Our first day at work was not a smooth one. Many men were slapped around or had to stand and hold a piece of railroad iron over their heads. This camp was standard procedure—like all the others. There was constant yelling. We were to always hurry, to work faster, and there was a constant effort to pit one American crew against another. Sticking together became even more crucial. We decided that if there were five cars on one sidetrack, every crew loading a car would work at the same speed. If one crew was slower because the guys were sick or physically unable to keep up, all other cars were kept waiting until they had finished their job. At that point, the Japs would start hollering. Sometimes a Jap would beat the sick crew who couldn't keep up.

The more work you did, the more they wanted you to do. The Japs were never satisfied. They needed us to finish each project so that they could use the docks to repair ships that our submarines had damaged. But we did everything possible to slow the work down. We were starved and sick, and they treated us like animals. Why in the world would we work faster, even if we could?

My buddy Roger usually worked as one of the winch operators or flagmen at the top of one of the dry docks where POWs loaded dirt and rocks. If the Japs were not right there watching between the winch operator and the flagman, these workers would hook the last car to the cable so that when the last car went over the top, the pin would jump out, which caused all the cars to rush down into the pit tearing up the tracks and dismantling most of the cars. That trick would cause a couple hours' delay.

The same technique could be used when the cars were being pulled out of the pit after being loaded. When the first car went over the top hump, the pin would jump out and the rest of the loaded cars would plunge to the bottom, severely damaging most of them. Once while the damage caused by of one of our sabotages was being repaired, Hitler was standing up on top yelling at everyone. As he was yelling, the winch operator noticed that he was standing inside the loop of a winch cable that was lying on the ground. He said nothing to anyone, but let the cable, which went up to a portable boom, tighten around Hitler's legs and feet, which then jerked him upside down and dropped him several feet on his head. He was taken away to the hospital.

It was done so slickly that no one could prove the winch operator knew what he had been doing. The first thing the operator did was stop the winch and go over to the crowd of Japs and say he was sorry. But it didn't matter whether it was an accident or had been done on purpose, they stood him at attention, slapped him around, and made him hold a piece of railroad iron over his head until he dropped. Then they kicked him. It was amazing what our men would risk in order to sabotage any effort of the enemy.

Loading and pushing the cars on narrow gauge rails was always dangerous. At one time, one of our guys had to be taken to the hospital because his left foot had been smashed around the ankle area. When he came back, we saw that the Jap doctor had cut his leg off at the hip joint, making it impossible for him to ever be fitted with an artificial leg.

Diarrhea was another problem. Everyone had diarrhea, and there were only three places the POWs could relieve themselves on the big projects. So most of the time, there was a long line at the benjos (toilets). At times, the work would come to a complete standstill because so many workers were lined up at the benjo. The Japs would go to the line, start yelling and insisting that each man did not have to go. So…we pulled down our pants and just went where we stood. "No, no, no…" the Japs would say and walk off in disgust. We would do anything we could to slow down the work.

As we were getting "adjusted" to this new place, we discovered that here again, our military guards would change about every two weeks. And again, most of these Japs had had been in combat and were delighted to take their anger out on us. Everyone's life was at risk 24 hours a day. Sometimes they came to our barracks, as many as five or six during the night, and would yell and drag us out because our shoes were not lined up straight. It was a terrible experience—the fear of not knowing when it will be your turn to be pulled out and beaten for no good reason. I was never sure I would live through another day, although I did everything I could think of to keep my life out of danger.

It didn't take long to get to know some of the other Americans who had joined us there. Although I wasn't able to make many close friends at Osaka #1 Camp, I thought it was important that I have some friends here. The first POWs I met were Ralph, Roger, Clyde (who we called Sam), and Mack; and we got to know each other well.

As there was at every other camp, there would be a few POWs here who also tried to get in good with the Japs and would do just about anything to be treated with favor. These men would even inform on other American prisoners which caused some of us to be beaten nearly to death. Even one of the officers was known as a "Jap lover." Some of us decided to "put these guys on notice." I was never convinced that it did any good.

Another morning came. A day like yesterday. Work…and loneliness…and pain…and hunger…. But this day would define the beginning of a different season.

It was about 10:30 a.m., and to our astonishment, the air raid alarm went off. Soon we heard high-flying bombers in the distance. High clouds covered most of the area, and within 20 minutes, the sky was buzzing with the noise of Jap planes. We also started hearing the blast of machine guns. Now we were sure that the Jap Zeros were firing on the B-29s. We also heard what we thought was the sound of a different type of machine gun coming from the high-flying bombers.

Minutes later we heard what sounded like a plane diving. At the same time, the Japs were jumping up and down, shouting, "B-29! B-29!" We did not see what kind of plane it was, but it fell not far away, and we could hear it hit the ground. Soon, smoke came up over the top of the hill. During this entire episode, every American was busting with joy, but no one made a sound or a reaction. There would be definite consequences to pay if we showed any hint of pleasure that American bombers had arrived. The next time, on our way to camp, we had to go over that hill. When we looked in the direction of where the plane had crashed, we all saw the tail section sticking up from the ground and on it was…a big…red… rising sun! Hallelujah! Then the guards got real mean, furious that the crashed airplane was one of their own. But it was obvious too that they were nervous.

That night we got very little sleep. Several of the guards came into our barracks, forcing us to get up so that they could take another count—as if we were planning to escape. Then the next day, the guards even told us how to take shelter when an air raid went into effect. We had heard rumors of American B-29s making raids on Tokyo, and now I was really hoping to see them for myself. Even though our lives would be at the same risk as the Japanese, this was one happy day.

My injured knee where I had been sliced by a bayonet at Osaka #1 Camp still bothered me. The weather was turning cold, and I felt I was coming down with malaria again. So I asked for light detail work. About 10 to 15 men were assigned to cleaning duty around the project and around the area where the small submarines were being built. At this area, there was a fence where elderly Japanese women and some children would come to watch the prisoners working. At times, they would come close enough to talk to some of us POWs. They were kind and would give us some parched beans that we shared among us.

There was one prisoner, though, who didn't care about anyone but himself. Somehow, this guy, not injured or sick that I could tell, had also managed to be assigned to the light detail. As an old lady motioned for someone to come to the fence, he went over and accepted a bag of parched beans from her. But when he walked back to our group, he refused to split the beans with any of us. This was totally unacceptable, and he and I got into an argument. He ended up saying that if anyone thought they could take them from him, they should "come on." I stepped up and tried to reason with him, but had no luck. Since we were on our lunch break eating our rice ball, there was no guard close by. This scoundrel called me a few foul names, and before I could move, he hit me pretty hard, knocking me backwards. My right knee gave in and I fell to my knees. A piece of gravel about the size of a marble stuck into the old bayonet wound and the blow caused blood to spray everywhere. When the guard came around, I told him that I had fallen. I also told the guy who hit me that I would settle with him later.

Our American doctor had no medical instruments to work with and had to fish the gravel out of the wound with his fingers and a pocketknife. He said that the knee was badly bruised, and by the next morning, my knee was so swollen that I could not stand. I was put in the sick bay where I began running a fever that turned into pneumonia. This was the second time I would have pneumonia in Japan.

Soon the knee got worse, and became badly infected. A Jap came by with Dr. Campbell to take a look and said that if the knee didn't get better soon, they would send me to the hospital and take off the leg. I immediately thought of the man whose ankle had been crushed and begged Dr. Campbell to please do something.

The Doc had an idea. He and I agreed that he would open the wound and pour pure iodine in it, let it sit for a while, then mash out any infected tissue the iodine would loosen up. Without giving me anything to deaden my knee, he took a regular pocketknife and cut it open while I held a cup to catch the blood and the pus. It was a cold day, but I was covered in sweat while watching the doctor cut on the wound. This process had to be done every twelve hours. At one point, when we saw some green-looking stuff come out of the wound, we knew blood poisoning was setting in. Still, the doctor told the Japs that I was getting better.

Eight inches below and above my knee, the skin was black and blue. The only place on my leg that had the sight of normal flesh was about one inch on the back. Again, I was in so much pain… but Dr. Campbell could actually see some improvement. I stayed in sick bay for about 30 days.

Then one morning, someone came in and announced that they had a cup of soup for each of the 28 men who were there. They started serving the sickest patient first. When everyone had been given a cup, they started over. That's when it sunk into my head that I was in bad shape. I was the second one they served! When I looked at number-one, I knew I had to get out of there.

The next day, number-one died. I could not walk, but I was determined to start crawling around the room, dragging the old bad knee and leg. Someone asked what the heck I was doing. I said, "I'm going back to work!" That's when the rest of them called me crazy. But then, three days later, number-three died. By then, I was pulling up and trying to stand on my leg. It took me another month but I eventually got well enough to get back on the sick detail that cleaned up the area.

As we watched the Japs who worked on the submarines, we started talking about what would happen if we were able to loosen the blocks that kept the unfinished submarine from sliding down into the water. So, every time we got close enough, we would bump the blocks a little more. We did this while the riveting guns were making their noise, so those working inside the submarine could not hear us bumping the blocks. Over and over, every chance we got, we continued to bump the blocks. Then one morning when we came to work, we were rewarded with a satisfying sight—our submarine was out in the bay—bottom up.

We were always constantly thinking and conniving about what we could do next to disrupt the work, and I was usually part of the scheme. I had reached the point where I could hobble, and they had moved me back to loading cars where we dug out dirt and rocks from the side of the hill. On this particular day, the tugboat taking the dumpster barge out to the bay was late coming back. So all the POWs, who had already loaded their cars and pushed them to the boat ramp, sat down and waited.

The Japs were not looking, so we decided to push all the cars we could onto the ramp, butt to butt, to see how many we could put on the ramp before it fell in. We put as many cars as there was room for—back to the bank and up to where the ramp hooked onto the land. As we worked, the dock began to crack.

There was room for one last car. We pushed hard and hit the car in front of it causing all the cars to move a notch. And that's all it took. The dock went into the bay—cars, tracks, and all. That sure slowed the entire project down. But that was also when we found out what real beatings were all about. Every man got it. Then they forced some of the men into the cold water to fish the pieces out of the water. We all expected them to shoot us.

At another time, we noticed that a huge dirt shovel had been placed at the front of our camp. It was somewhat like a steam shovel, but fully electric, operating on tank tracks. We assumed it was to be used on the project somewhere, and were told that it had come from England. In fact, we could see the name and English writing on it.

During one of the cleanups around the camp, a Navy electrician was able to get into the control box when the guard couldn't see him and cross-wired it. When they decided to move it, smoke suddenly came out of it and the big motor died. It never did move again.

Our "stealing anything of value" program was also still in effect—wire wrenches, tools, anything. We'd carry the items back to the camp and then throw them into our slit trench in the benjo. Soon, though, it came time when the Japs called for a honey wagon (that's what we called it) to clean out our slit trench. That's when they discovered what had happened to all the missing items.

They spread all the items out and ordered us to walk by and pick out the ones we had personally stolen. No one would point at anything, and no one would rat on anyone else. So again, we all got a lesson on the evil of stealing and destroying things of value.

At times, the cement for the mixer was brought into the project by a wagon that was pulled by a big ox. One day the wagon came in with a heavy load. The Jap who drove the ox was yelling at it and beating it unmercifully. And the ox had had enough. It stopped and would not or could no longer pull the wagon up a small incline. Even with all the yelling and beating, he still would not move. He was just…done. So the Jap unhooked the ox from the wagon, tied him to a tree, and went over the hill talking to himself. Soon he returned with a bigger ox, hooked him up to the wagon, and over the hill the wagon went. Later, we noticed the Jap returning to where the first ox had been tied to the tree. This time, he took the ox's head and tied it sideways tight up to the tree. He got out his lunch box and sat right in front of the ox and ate his lunch. He proceeded to admonish the old animal, adamantly declaring that the beast was not going to get anything to eat because he had not pulled the wagon over the hill. We all could relate to how the ox felt. I'm sure it understood as much as we did when we first were captured and tried to understand or figure out what the Japs wanted us to do.

In time, we heard that American B-29s were regularly bombing places like Osaka, Kobe, and other cities nearby. Again, even though we realized that there was a high probability that we would become targets as well, our spirits couldn't help but to lift. We understood there was no way that Americans could know where the Japs had taken us. We just wanted the Japs to get what they deserved. We wanted justice—the same treatment that they had extended to us.

But with still no definite end in sight, my friend Clyde, like all of us, was just about fed up. He wondered how much longer he could last. When would he get beaten to death? Or now…maybe a bomb would kill him. He was even thinking about trying to take a gun away from a guard and kill as many Japs as he could before they killed him. I completely understood and knew just how he felt. At times, I also had the same thoughts. But this guy was *very* serious. Even though I sympathized, I was starting to feel better and attempted to talk some sense into him. For about a week, I took every chance I could to talk to him and watched him much of the time in case he decided to carry out any of his threats. It took a good two weeks to change his thinking, and finally he realized that maybe we might survive and go home.

Again, I would think about what Howard Leachman had said to me on the Tayabas Road detail and would remember his premonition—"You're the only one here that I know who will make it home…." I don't know why, but that prediction kept coming back to me, and it gave me hope, which most of the time, was the only thing I had to cling to. I tried to get Clyde to think that way, too. Fortunately, for some reason, he gave up on his plans.

I had another friend, Roger, who was always optimistic and full of hope. He looked like he was managing as well as anyone. When some of the men tried to divide us up by pitting one group against another, Roger would tell them he wanted no part of it. Whatever their game was, Roger was not playing it. He said his friends were going to stay his friends. He claimed that this was no time to create faction among ourselves. Our real and only enemy was the Japs. I always admired him for his stand and the many other fine qualities he displayed.

Then there was Ralph, a fellow Alabamian. He and I would sit when we had the chance and talk about what we were going to cook up and eat when we got back home. Even a bowl of chitlins sounded good at this point. Ralph could make a steak sound so good that I could just about taste it. He would call me a fellow "hog poler." When I asked him what a "hog poler" was, he said that in the hills of northern Alabama, there were not many fields to feed the hogs, so they would put the hogs on a pole and hold them up against the hill so that they could eat what acorns they could find on the side of the hill.

Another friend, Mack, was always there to help anyone. He was from Arkansas. He could do almost anything; but in prison, the Japs wanted him to cook. And Mack didn't know anything about cooking. I don't believe he could boil water without burning it. But he was a true believer that somehow we would all get out. I guess he hated the Japs as much as any of us.

In time, we had messed up the project site about as much as we could without getting shot. Now, we were determined to accomplish the biggest caper of all. Our plan was to move a large rock across the yard and into the hopper so that it broke the blades of the big cement mixer. If we could manage to do this, the project would no doubt close for an extended time. The size of the rock needed to accomplish such an endeavor would be hard for us to lift, but we were committed to it.

This job—moving the rock all the way across the project and into the hopper—took more than two months. At one point, a Jap noticed this particular rock and had some men load the rock into one of the cars, but by luck we were able to get it back out and start moving it again toward the mixer area.

In the meantime, the Japs were starting to pour the cement locks for the front of the dry docks, so it also became imperative that we do everything we could to mess up the cement that went into the forms. The forms held the doors that, in turn, held back the water pressure from the bay as a ship was being repaired inside. These doors were about eight feet thick and reinforced with steel. To weaken the cement, we put in wood, trash, sand, and other materials that would make the cement crack when pressure was applied. But the materials that were added couldn't be seen in the cement. When the forms were removed, the cement still had to look good and smooth. In order to accomplish all this, we decided that when the cementing started, we had to create a diversion by attacking each other. Others would then throw the materials in and cover them up before the Japs could see what we had done.

As we got close to finishing the first forms, we hoped we could get that big rock into the sand hopper before we had to start on the next forms. While we worked, the Jap prisoners next door told one of our men that they had been working on this same project for over ten years. The guards treated them about the same as they treated us, and many times we would hear screams coming from their camp.

We always had to be very careful whom we told about "the rock." There was one particular American officer who we knew would tell the Japs if he found out the plan. It was a good day when we got word that the rock was now in the hopper and in the right place to go straight to the mixer. We couldn't wait! For some time, it looked as if it might never get there.

Then, about 3 p.m., the company whistle blew. That meant assembly time for the POWs. The Japs were buzzing around, and many of us knew what was coming. There were some POWS who hadn't been involved in this scheme and had no clue as to what was happening. And no one who did know would tell them anything.

We were ordered to return to the camp, and it was just about quitting time by the time we got there. All guards were standing outside along with all the Jap bosses. The Japanese commander and the man who was in charge of the cement hopper were also there as we lined up. They made us stand at arm's length from each other and then began questioning some of the men. This time, we definitely needed to stick together.

Yet soon, I heard one POW saying it was not fair to kill all of us for what a few might have done. As the Japs tried to find out who was responsible, the rest of took the position that we knew nothing. The Americans who actually had nothing to do with it were telling the truth. The ones who were responsible certainly were not going to say anything. We stayed lined up for eight hours until 11 p.m., and there was no dinner rice.

Many men were beaten and some were taken into the commander's office. All of us were praying that no one would break and reveal the truth. Thank God, no one gave in. I'm glad we weren't there when the locks were tested.

Almost daily now we could hear the American B-29s coming closer to us, and many times, we could see them flying over us. They looked as though they were about 50 or 60 thousand feet high. Word was that they were burning out towns and killing many women and children. We didn't know for sure but figured it would just be a matter of time before the B-29s hit our area. Would that mean the end for us as well?

The Japs were masters at keeping news from us and also from the working class and general population. The only account we were given was that the Japs were winning. But when new Army guards arrived, we somehow sensed conditions were getting worse for them by the way they treated us. Once in a while, the guards would refer to the B-29s as being "very bad" for them.

I had been a prisoner of war for about two and one-half years. At 20 years of age, it had been a lifetime of slavery—an eternity of horror—killings, beatings, sickness, starvation, and pain.

I reached the point of expecting nothing…and thoughts of the war coming to an end were still just an imagination. I couldn't remember what it was like to be free. *Was it a dream I once had? Had I ever had a good night's sleep without worrying about being beaten to death before the sun came up? Had I ever had to refuse food because my stomach was simply stuffed? Had I ever walked leisurely and spontaneously where I wanted to? Had I ever felt the comfort of clean clothing without the constant reminder of bugs crawling against my body? Had I ever experienced one day completely free of physical pain? Was there ever a time that I simply smiled at everyone passing by and could expect the kindness in return?* I had learned that real life was more than material possessions. Freedom and good health was the greatest gifts from God, and I would never take them for granted if I ever had the chance to enjoy them again.

I did have one last hope—the B-29s. I would daydream that America would bomb and kill every last Jap and that maybe…just some way…some of us could escape. If I did not survive, I would be satisfied that the Japs got what they deserved.

Towards the end of 1944 we were to be moved again. There was only a handful of belongings to grab. No one would miss this rock pile.

10

KOBE GRAPHITE FACTORY

We had no idea where we were headed as we loaded onto the trucks, then transferred to a train. Our guards were very careful not to tell anyone where the train was going. Had we been able to read Japanese, we might have known we were in Kobe when we arrived in September 1944. Our concern about B-29s hitting the rock pile was nothing compared to the strain we were now faced with. This place—with all its factories and an airstrip in front of the building where we unloaded—was just the kind of target that B-29s would be looking for.

When I looked at Roger and Clyde, I knew they were thinking the same thing. I hoped our barracks would be at a safe distance from this part of our new headquarters, but it wasn't to be. We were taken to our new living quarters that were a part of the big building by the airstrip. It was obvious—this place was a perfect bomb target, and we were sitting ducks. As I looked at each man's face, I could see the realization—the disappointment and the fear.

Our food was about the same as before, and we were watched by the same civilian guards. How I wished we could get rid of the one we called "the emperor." At one time or another, he had beaten just about every man for no good reason at all. I think he took out his personal frustrations on us. Sir Baloney Bird was not as bad as long as we addressed him as "Sir Baloney Bird." When we called him that, he would

157

throw back his shoulders and sort of strut as if he were someone important. For some reason, he considered the title a great compliment.

When we went to work the next morning after we arrived, we were startled to discover what we would be making. The building was full of various sizes of extruders to produce graphite cores for dry cell batteries. I soon realized that the large ones were to be used in suicide submarines. This meant that we would be directly responsible for making part of a weapon whose purpose would be to kill other Americans. This was in flagrant violation of the Geneva Code, and greatly bothered all of us.

When the graphite cores came out of the extruder, some smaller ones would be soft and would have to sit and cure. Most of the larger cores were hard. An inspector would mark them as good or bad, and the bad ones would be returned to be recycled. The good ones went to an area to be stacked for shipping. With all the handling and access we had to the cores, we POWs were able to damage some of the good ones. We also soon discovered a few ways to slow down the production. Since there were no additional inspections after the first one, we were able to wipe out the approval markings stamped on by the inspector, and then place the good batteries into the defective bin. We cut production by 50 to 100 batteries the first month.

It wasn't long before we heard that the B-29s were coming closer... and closer. Everyone was concerned about the possibility of being hit, and we had to figure out how we were going to get out of this place.

One day, one of the guys had what the doctor thought was a stroke or an epilepsy attack. He was foaming at the mouth, kicking, and rolling on the ground. None of the Japs would get close to him, and they told our cook to put him in sick bay. The thought occurred to us that this little episode might just give us a way to get out of here. When the Japs asked what we thought was wrong with him, we decided to tell them that he had a tropical disease and that it was contagious. We noticed that the guards wouldn't dare go to the sick bay again.

We found out, too, that one of the buildings was full of wheat. In addition, we figured out a way to prepare and cook it by pulling up the floorboards and putting a can of charcoal between the floor and the ground. It was hard, though, to get into the storage building to steal the wheat. So Mack and I had to discover a way to get past the guard who would walk from one side of the building to the other. When he turned to go away from us, we ran across the drive to the backside of the building with the wheat and then went through a window. Then we made our way back across the drive and stashed the wheat for a later pickup.

We continued to do this for a while. But at one time, as we were crossing the drive, the guard happened to notice us and started running towards us. Mack went in one direction and I went in another. The guard chose to follow me. I ran around a building, and just as I turned the corner I saw five POWs digging a small drainage ditch. One of the workers had gone to the benjo and his shovel was lying on the ground. I grabbed it up and started digging. When the Jap came around the corner, I pointed to another building. He took off running. I dropped the shovel and went immediately back to my job, only to get slapped for taking so long at the benjo.

Later when we cooked the wheat, we found that the wheat was soaked with napalm from a recent B-29 attack. It made us sick. One guy swelled up twice his size. His belly stuck out so far he could not stoop over. We joked and told him not to point his rear end at us! And with graphite everywhere around us, each of us eventually looked as though we had been painted black. Because there was not enough soap to remove the stains, some of the men tried using sand. They managed to get rid of some of the graphite, but still, all of us were black.

The battery production was now down from 300 a month when we arrived to fewer than 100 a month. The Japs were getting upset and demanded that all the POWs stay away from the machines.

They also started running more inspections to determine if anyone was damaging the sticks. But by now, we could still do the same things, just in different ways. The guards would knock us around, but even so, they did not have a sufficient number of inspectors to keep us from damaging the batteries. Consequently, the production numbers remained low.

In the meantime, the B-29s were coming even closer. We could hear the bombs explode and could see that an area not far from us was on fire. That's when we decided we really had to get out of there. We decided we all would start having seizures, but not too many at the same time. One night, someone even came up with the idea of faking his own hanging. The guards asked us why the man had tried to hang himself. We told them that he was starting to get the tropical disease like the POW had who had been foaming at the mouth. This really scared them, and they wouldn't touch this POW either.

Most of the time we continued to act crazy and "have seizures," continually insisting that all our symptoms were due to "some tropical disease" or perhaps the building we were working was dangerous for everyone's health in some way. They did not know what to do with us.

At the end of three months, the Japs were convinced that we all had gone mad, and the Jap workers were afraid to work with us. The production was down to nothing, and we had become useless to them. So once again, we were told that we would be moved.

The morning we lined up to leave, a Marine who could understand Japanese heard two Japs talking. They were still trying to decide if we had been faking a lot of the craziness and illness. We held our breath. Lucky for us, the Jap workers really wanted us out of there, and they decided that it was too late to change their minds.

11

TSURAGA

From Kobe we were now on our way to Tsuraga, our fourth Japanese POW camp since we had arrived in Japan in November 1942. We were discouraged, going through the motions…just existing. This winter of '44-45 would be brutal, like all the previous winters, and the summer would be almost unbearable. There was always so much suffering—very little food, the bare minimum of protection from the weather, inadequate medicine…we were walking skeletons with barely a hope left in the world.

Looking back, my time as a prisoner of war is hard to describe, and I can scarcely believe that any of us survived this miserable way of life—if you could even call it "life." Our bodies were still moving, but our minds had become numb. We stumbled through each day just trying not to think. If we dwelled on the horror at hand, we would have to fight a severe battle of depression and discouragement. You had to tell yourself that you weren't hungry, that you didn't hurt…you had to remind yourself that you didn't want any space or need any privacy. The only privacy you had were those thoughts inside your own mind. Yet you had to stay away from that really deep, dark place. We realized we needed each other, if only to reassure the next guy that he was still alive.

There was not one of us who had not been beaten and beaten…
and beaten—over and over again. And still, each beating was so
hard to take. When a man loses a fight in a barroom brawl, he
can usually handle any shame or embarrassment that might come
along in the aftermath of it, and just simply move on; but this
type of relentless beating—the cruel torture that we had to endure,
suffering the indignity of having to stand there and take it—was
the ultimate humiliation. While you are suffering indescribable
pain, you are sick with the thought that you can do nothing about
it—not raise your hands or your feet or any part of your body in
defense. You want to silently bear each blow; you don't want to give
the attacker any type of satisfaction as each rifle butt is jammed
into your stomach, and slammed into your back, and pounded into
your head, and then again to your back…over…and over…and
over. But then…a gasp, or a moan, or even a scream escapes from
your lips. You are totally…helpless.

You collapse there, but want so much to stand back up and spit
on your attacker. You want to curl your hands around his revolting
neck and squeeze until all the frustration has gone out of you and
all the life has gone out of him. You don't want him to simply die;
you want him to suffer—to suffer forever; you want to inflict the
most pain, spill the most blood…but most of all, you want to see
his eyes as they reflect the horror, the surprise, the ultimate realization
that *he is going to die*…and that…*you are the one who will kill him.*

Seeing my friends, my comrades, other American soldiers being beaten, was at times even worse than suffering my own fate,
especially if that man was too sick or too weak to make it through
another beating. As he would jerk with each slam against his body,
I could feel each blow against my own. And even more devastating
was that we *had* to watch—we had to just…watch. We couldn't
help. What agony it was to not be able to simply…help. How in
the name of God could we just stand there as trained soldiers and
not provide some sort of protection? But if we dared move to assist

in any way, to show any hint of sympathy, we made it worse—we just made it worse for the poor soul suffering on the ground.

I would ask over and over, *How can another human being be so fiercely cruel, be so inhuman, so ruthless?* I experienced an outrage like none other as I observed these bloodthirsty Japs completely ignore the horrible and painful condition of our men and continue to beat on and on with such hatred and scorn. It was depraved. It was evil. It was from the pits of hell.

We had now been POWs for almost three years. Three years. Many times, I didn't think about the war ending. It had been such a long time now. It was hopeless. There was no way we would ever go home, and there was no use in dreaming of ways we could possibly get out alive. I would probably die in these despicable surroundings, and most of the other men felt the same. We would ask, "Why have I fought so hard to survive, if it has been only to suffer this brutal treatment, this hideous existence, and the end result is still death? Wouldn't it have been better had I died at the beginning of the Death March and escaped all this terror and torture?"

But…still…there was this one small glimmer of hope that we all were desperately clinging to—the B-29s. I was convinced that there was no way the US forces could defeat the Japs except to invade their homeland. This meant that we prisoners of war might be killed also, but we still held on to this hope. Every now and then, we had heard that the B-29s were continuing to bomb Japan, and that the Japanese were feeling the effects of it. The prisoners knew firsthand how constant bombing, sooner or later, overwhelms the victims. The Japanese were definitely suffering under the strain of a daily threat of danger and destruction, and from the fear that they might die during the next raid. We did not feel sorry for them.

When we had left the Kobe Graphite Factory, we had been marched to the railroad station to be loaded onto a train. As we walked on through the station, a Jap came out one of the doors and asked the following questions in English: "How many prisoners are traveling in your group? … What camp have you come from? … Where are you going?" We wondered, *Do these questions mean that someone from the USA knows about us? Someone is thinking about us?*

At this low point of our lives, wanting desperately to hope but yet afraid to, we were a little comforted that our government might be more aware of our circumstances than we had thought. Beforehand, most of us had seriously considered that Tokyo Rose, the voice we had heard on the radio in Bataan, might have been right when saying that we would not be welcomed back to the USA. And after all we had been through, physically and mentally, it was impossible not to doubt if the people back home still cared about us. Most of us hadn't heard from home, and we had been slaves for such a long time—long enough to be convinced that we were unloved and unwanted by everyone—including our own families.

Now, after years in bondage, my thoughts about home were no longer the same as they had been during the first part of the war. When I was first captured, I still thought often about my girlfriend, my family, and my childhood friends as they had been when I had left them. Now, years later, too much time had passed. Not only had I changed, they would have changed as well. *How would they really feel about me now? Would they even want me around?* I began to think about not going home at all. If my family had received word that my dog tags had been found in the mass grave at Camp O'Donnell, they would have accepted my death by now and moved on with their lives. *Why should I show up and disrupt their families, possibly giving them more grief? I should just go somewhere else and let them believe I had died at Camp O'Donnell.*

Soon the train we were riding in entered a valley. I could see a port, an out-of-the-way-type place, surrounded by mountains. In the midst of so much despair, it looked...peaceful, and with it came a flicker of desire, a sudden rise of hope that we were coming to a place and time that would bring this dreadful experience to an end.

As I watched the ships sailing in and out of the harbor, I immediately thought that we might be unloading some of those ships, and if so, here was a possibility of handling...*food*. And maybe, we might be able to smuggle some of it into camp. What would it feel like to have a full stomach for a change, and then say, "No more, thank you. I've had plenty to eat"?

It was sometime in December 1944 when we arrived at our new quarters. The "Emperor" and "Sir Baloney Bird," our civilian guards, were still with us; and the camp commander gave the same old speech—"Obey orders or be punished. You are a guest of the Emperor while here in Japan." We moved in—it was the same living conditions. Who expected that things would be any better?

Our rice ration was about the same as at the last camp, soggy with a few black-eyed worms. I weighed about 125 pounds and was a walking corpse...we all were. And I was still moving around with a limp, a result of the bayonet wound I had suffered in Osaka. We brought along the body lice, and I thought back to the time when our interpreter told us in Tanagawa that he didn't want us "sleeping with the bear" and "making trouble with the fleas."

As we lined up for our work assignment the next morning, the north wind coming off the water cut right through the old Jap uniform I had been given to wear. The cement paper I was using to stop the wind from freezing me to death was about worn out and helped very little to keep me warm.

Just as I and other prisoners had expected, we would be unloading ships. We were marched to the docks where several ships were tied up, and there we met our new Japanese bosses. One, who acted like he had been gifted with a little more authority than the others, was a Jap about five-feet, nine-inches tall with long legs and a short body. It didn't take long to name him "Bird Legs." The other boss—well, he was wearing a baseball cap with the bill turned up. We named him "Simple Simon."

The bosses separated us into groups of 20 to 30 men. My first job was cleaning up the mess in a long warehouse along the dock, at which four ships could pull up to at once. As far as I could determine, some ships were coming from Manchuria and were loaded with bags of rice, soybeans, and boxes of dried fish. Other ships carried machinery and steel railroad irons.

The bags of beans and rice were to be carried from the ships and then stacked in the warehouse where they would be reloaded into railroad cars that ran on a railroad siding along the length of the warehouse. As soon as we got there, we noticed that there were some beans and rice spilled on the floor. We were told to scoop them up and put them in a container that looked like a garbage can. We were not permitted to eat any of the beans or rice, and if we did, we would be punished. Within minutes, I had a mouthful of raw beans. If a Jap asked me a question while I was trying to chew, I simply swallowed the beans whole before answering. One of the prisoners couldn't help but to ask if any B-29s had been seen in Tsuraga and or had done any damage. In short order, he was slapped a few times and told, "No B-29s in Tsuraga!" We were glad to hear that good news for our own safety.

Soon we met our new interpreter. His English was adequate enough, but there was something different about this one. He actually had very little to say to us at first. He was quiet and very unlike the other interpreters had been. When we got back to the barracks that night, the men were talking. The interpreter had told some of them that he had been born in America—in Cleveland, Ohio. He and his family had come to Japan to visit some extended family members before the war had begun. Once the war had started, though, the Japanese government had kept them from returning to the States. As the guys continued talking about this interpreter, they mentioned that he was already showing some interest in our conditions and our circumstances, and would not be looking for excuses to have a guard beat us.

On the other hand, the Japs didn't trust this interpreter, and most of the time posted a guard to follow him closely, wherever he went. The interpreter acknowledged that he had very little influence with the Japs and was limited as to what he could do, but would help us whenever he could, which made us all feel a little better. Indeed, he eventually proved his worth to us in various ways. When we realized that this inland port, though small in size, was a very important one for supplying food to all of Japan, we decided that we would have to slow down the flow of food to the rest of the country. The interpreter heard about our "delay-and-destroy program" and assured us that this plan would be a snap to put into place here at Tsuraga.

Again, we had to make our intentional destruction look like accidents. As soon as we caused a disruption, we learned to run to the nearest Jap guard and say, "*Sumie my sin*," meaning, "I'm sorry," to allay their suspicions. At first, this plan worked well, but ultimately, there had been too many "Sumie my sin's," which meant that we were watched all the more closely and didn't have as many opportunities to make our "mistakes."

Meanwhile, one of the Japanese bosses came around with the interpreter to tell us that they wanted some Navy men to run the winches that would pull the nets of bags out of the hold of the ship and move them to the dock side of the warehouse. He admitted that they wanted to relieve the Jap winch operators so that these operators could report and fight for the Japanese army. That was the worst thing they could have told us. We sure weren't about to "relieve" anyone so they would be free to help fight our men.

As the Japs went around to recruit "volunteers," all the Navy men insisted that they had served in the military as cooks. In the end, the Japs demanded that four of the men get on the ships and proceeded to show them how to operate the winches and booms. When the first American tried to unload the first net, he pulled it up all the way to the top end of the ship's boom. Then he moved it from side to side, and then let the net down about halfway. The heavy net kept swinging from side to side and broke one of the side ropes, which caused a bag to sling all the way out over the water. When the net went swinging toward the warehouse, two bags of food came out of the net like a missile, shooting one bag through the roof of the warehouse. The other bag hit the side of the warehouse and burst, with the rice going all over the place. About five Japs began yelling. Before they could stop it, though, the net hit the ship's rails, tearing them down as well. The balance of the load from the net went back down in the hold of the ship with a big bang.

When they finally were able to drag the POW away from the winch controls, he again told them he was a cook and did not know how to run a winch. While this whole drama was somewhat humorous, the beating that followed was not. Still, the other men continued to prove that they also had similar problems with operating the winch. One pulled the net to the top, mashing the clutch and letting it freefall back into the ship's hold. It just about knocked the bottom out of the ship. Bird Legs stood by shaking his head and saying, "You have sorry Navy. Japanese—very good with winch." He also had to add that American cooks didn't know how to cook rice. We shrugged our shoulders and looked stupefied. And our Navy men no longer operated the winches.

As we worked, there were Japanese citizens who also worked alongside us, and who wore belly bands to keep their stomachs warm. Each day, many of these Japs would use these bands to hide and carry out stolen rice and beans. Ironically, it was part of their duty to help the Army guards check the POWs as we left to go to our barracks at the end of the day. When they searched us and found rice or beans in our pockets, we would casually touch their belly band, look straight in their eyes, and say, "Momeys." (beans). Those Japs knew that we knew they were also stealing. We all knew that they, as well, would be severely punished if they were caught. So, these guys would just pass by us and go on down the line without reporting anything to the Jap guard on duty. This meant we all were able to get more rice and beans back into the camp, and this was more food than we had received for a long time! And even a little more food certainly helped the sick.

We found out that if we ate a combination of rice, onions, and orange peelings, we could produce an interesting amount of personal gas; and when we passed this gas, anyone around us would quickly move in another direction. We used our malodorous wind like the skunks use theirs against an attacker. If a Jap started towards us, any American could let the Jap have it. In every case, that Jap would leave in a hurry.

Actually, most of the POWs started to feel better and were getting stronger and appeared to be in better shape. We were able to find and eat more beans and rice, even stashing some in our sleeping area. In fact, it wasn't long before I was put on the detail of moving bags from the warehouse to the trains. Even though the Japs were somewhat better workers on this detail than we were, we Americans held our own and many of us were able to carry a 100-pound bag on our back from the warehouse, up a plank, and into the rail car.

Fortunately, in several small ways, we were able to keep delaying and destroying their food supply; we felt that every little setback helped the American cause. Their railroad cars, small compared to our American cars, were to be loaded with 380 bags in each car. So…we simply piled several of the bags higher at the door than were piled further inside the car. The short Jap inspector would come by, glance at the car from his position on the ground, and then ask, "380 bags?" We would answer," Hei," meaning, "Yes."

The inspector then closed the door, put the car seal over the door lock, and went on to the next car.

But our job wasn't finished yet. We had to make it look like someone stole from the car after it left the yard, so before the train pulled the car out, we would cut the seal off the door. We never let a car out of the yard with a seal on a car that we had shortchanged.

We figured we were being relatively successful destroying their food supply, but this achievement brought on another problem. Rice and beans were now stacked up in the warehouse, and so we had to find a way to get rid of the abundance. Imagine that. We decided that while some guys started a fight inside the warehouse, causing the Japs to run inside, others of us would be at the dockside tossing the food bags into the bay. This worked for a while.

Then one morning, the tide was out, and a couple of ships could not get close enough to pull up dockside. So, the Japanese ordered a dredge to come and clear out the bay near the dock area. It took a couple of days to get it there, but when it finally arrived and began working, up came the bags of beans and rice. And again, every one of us who worked in that area were "reprimanded" physically and severely by the guards.

As for "Simple Simon," well, he turned out to be just as we had thought—simple. We could fool him about most anything. One time, when we were faking a fight among us, someone got close enough to Simon to knock his baseball cap bill back down. The next thing we knew, Simon's eyes went up and turned backwards into his head, and he had to be led away to the hospital.

Within a couple of weeks, Simon returned to work as our boss. But as soon as he started yelling at us, or doing something mean, we would fake a fight just so that we could get close enough to him to flip his cap bill down. Every time we did that, he was again taken away to stay in the hospital for another couple weeks! Bird Legs thought he would convince us to have some sympathy around Simon and to make sure to help Simon when he was having one of his fits. They never did figure out that we were flipping his cap bill down and were the cause of his fits in the first place.

We also found out that the guard was correct when he had said to us on our first day of arrival, "No B-29's in Tsuraga." From time to time, we would still hear rumors of bombings, but we couldn't dare to hope it was anything of significance.

After a couple of months, though, the air raid signal started to sound periodically. And sometimes we would hear planes, but could never spot any. The Japs would insist that the planes were over the mountains and would order us to keep working.

To warn everyone of an air raid, Bird Legs would beat on an iron, triangular-shaped device. If the air raid warning sounded off in short signals, that meant the planes were close, not just over the mountains, and might be flying over us. Then, if Bird Legs could see the planes, he would hit that device three times, in three separate signals, which alerted us to take cover. His signals were our only air raid warnings.

One day, we were ordered to come back into camp early. To our surprise the Japs had pulled an inspection of all the bunks. Each of our bunks had been marked with a number, and mine was 632. If they had found anything during the inspection that they thought you shouldn't have, they removed that item and put your number on it.

There were many things displayed on the table. All the men from the sick bay were lined up as well to be used as witnesses. The Jap guards proceeded to take each item that was marked with our bunk number, and in front of all the others, beat us with it until we could not stand up. Then they kicked us until we were too helpless to get up. When there were so many men on the floor, the Jap guards would drag some of them out of the way. I thought surely they were going to kill my friend Roger. Several of the items on the table had been marked with his bunk number. The next morning, the men who were in too much pain to go to work were beaten again.

Loading the rails was a hard job and many times dangerous. A boom was used to lift up the bundles of rails from the ground. Connected to the boom by two ropes was a small winch over the side of the gondolier. Each rope was held by one of two men. When the winch operator lifted up the bundle of rails, one man had to pull the boom over the top of the gondolier. Then the winch operator lowered the bundle onto the gondolier. The man inside the gondolier would unhook the cable, then signal to the winch man to pull the cable up to get it out from under the rails, then call clear in order to be ready for another bundle. The second man holding the other rope would then pull the boom back to the pile of rails on the ground. When the winch operator was pulling up the cable, sometimes the rails would shift, and anyone working in the gondolier had to be careful not to get hurt.

One day, we were unloading narrow gauge railroad tracks that had been shipped in from Manchuria, then reloading them on railroad gondoliers to be shipped out. There was a harsh supervisor in charge of our loading efforts, and he kept yelling at us. He especially was not satisfied as to how my friend Mack was working inside the gondolier, so he climbed inside to show Mack how to stack the tracks and keep them straight to make more room for a larger number of tracks to be loaded. He got the winch operator and Mack so confused that a bundle was shifted and accidentally crushed the guard into the wall of the gondolier. One of the bands used to connect the rails went into his groin and lower stomach area. We pulled the rails off him.

One of our crew ran and told Bird Legs what had happened. The injured Japanese guard was carried out and laid on the ground, his blood soaking through his pants. While waiting for someone to take him to the hospital, the Japanese just stood there, trying to look through the hole in his pants to see the extent of the injury, but made no effort to open his pants to stop the bleeding.

When the emergency equipment arrived, it turned out to be a three-wheeled bicycle with a basket on back. They loaded that guard into the basket with his head hanging over to one side. The Japs were all yelling for the bicycle operator to hurry up, and he took off as fast as he could with the tires running over the ends of the railroad ties.

As the Japs yelled, this man's head was bouncing up and down, hanging out of the basket. I think the ride is what killed him, not the loss of blood. To us, it was another dead Jap—out of the way. We felt no pity.

Although the air raid warnings were sounding more frequently, we still saw no planes flying directly over us. And so again, when Bird Legs started to beat on his iron contraption in the middle of the night, we expected to next hear the usual all-clear sound, telling us the danger was over. But this time, the short signals started, warning that the planes were in our area. As the guards were trying to get organized to take us out of the building, all of a sudden, we heard planes coming really close, and soon, bombs were raining down all over the town.

We had just managed to get out of the building and take cover, when our barracks caught fire. It was going up in flames along with all the other buildings around us. In an instant, my little handful of belongings went up in smoke as well. And I thought, *Well, what can you lose if you have nothing in the first place?*

Out of our 340 men, only one suffered a small burn on his face. Bird Legs, as well as some other guards, looked at us and said, "Your own country bombed you…but why didn't some of you get hit?" We explained that we had been through this drill before; we knew where to go and what to do in a bombing. After that, the Japs waited to see where we went during an air raid. You would have to run fast to get to a ditch or trench before three or four Japs would beat you there! During one raid, I ended up sprawled on top of Bird Legs and two other Japs.

Our barracks were gone. Everywhere, all you could see were the outlines of buildings. Ashes covered the ground, and you had to look carefully to see where other buildings had once stood. The guard, "Emperor," soon came around to head up a detail of us POWs who were to help clean up the area. We all hated the Emperor. So when one of our group found an old benjo slit trench among the rubble, he plotted a scheme, and stuck a stick down into the trench. It took some time, but we convinced the Emperor to move near the trench; and as he did, this guy called the Emperor to come see what he had found. The Emperor came walking straight towards him and walked right into the bingo slit trench, falling in up to his head. He was covered with POW crap! He crawled out yelling and screaming, while yanking his clothes off. By the time he got to the water, he was as naked as a jaybird. He was so mad he wanted to kill every one of us. Our friendly interpreter talked him out of it, saying the man who had summoned him honestly did not know exactly where the bingo slit trench was located. The great Emperor was never the same after that.

Sir Baloney Bird, on the other hand, continued to be very proud of his name, smiling and strutting whenever we addressed him. Then…he took a two-week leave. During the first formation after he returned, we noticed that he was not at all happy with us. After head counting was completed, he went to the front of the formation and in broken English, said, "I found out name—Sir Baloney Bird—jo to ni (*no good*)—never want to hear again." The interpreter was amused at us and at him, but he warned us not to give him a chance to beat us, because he might "take the beating to the end"—meaning our death. So we all were very careful after that and never let him hear us call him by his nickname again.

After our building was burned out, they moved us to an abandoned brick kiln on the edge of town across the street from a large clothing factory. The air raids began to pick up. Eventually, the warning would go off every 30 to 40 minutes. The planes did not always hit our area, but came close enough.

One day, we talked the Japanese into letting 50 men at a time wash our only clothes in salt water without soap—not very effective, but it gave us a day off. Our group had already washed our clothes, and the 50 of us naked men were waiting in the one end of a long warehouse for our clothes to dry. One of the guys with the artillery unit thought he heard something and went to check outside. Looking through his fingers at the sun, he started yelling, "Here they come—down 11 a.m.!"

We had no idea what he meant. Then he said, "Run...run!" Fifty men were trying to get through the door at one time, then across the railroad tracks and on over a long pile of coal. A guy by the name of Draper and I were the last to get to the door, and as we did, we saw the other 48 naked guys flying over that coal pile! I fell down laughing. Our Navy bombers were in full force. As I looked back, I could see fire all over the place, rockets going in every direction. We ran all the way to a small hill that overlooked the dock area.

Wave after wave of our Navy planes continued to fly overhead. Meanwhile, a Jap with a machine gun had stationed himself up in a ship's mast. He would wait for the planes to pull up after dropping their bomb loads and then would shoot at them. Fortunately, one of our Navy pilots spotted him and pulled up in a different direction. The Jap jumped out of the crow's nest and landed on the ship's deck. We never saw him move.

We were up there on that hill, yelling, jumping up and down like we were at a football game. What a wonderful sight! Soon the pilot saw us and must have realized we were American POWs. He gave his plane wings a couple of waves at us. After that, all the planes pulled up and went out over the port. I wish I could have heard what he reported about 50 naked American POWs on a hill, waving and jumping up and down.

That air raid did even more damage to that little port, and the Japs continued to take off whenever the air raid warnings sounded. Their attitude also got meaner towards us. At the same time, the interpreter would talk to us privately and expressed compassion for us. He even delivered some 16 mm movies to us so that we could realize how long the Japs had tried to turn their children against Americans. In these movies, monkeys were used to portray the Imperial Japanese race, while white pigs were shown as the Americans, proving to their children that they were the superior race.

In the meantime, American planes were bombing all over Japan. They kept coming right on schedule, about every 30 minutes. And our Jap bosses kept the pressure on.

It was now the end of July 1945, and one evening, I was standing outside and looking up at the night sky. What I saw took my breath away. There was the new moon, clear as could be—with no obstruction—no trees, no clouds, nothing in front of it—just the sight of the moon. I immediately remembered something my mother had told me when I was still a child. She said when you first saw the new moon, you could tell by the number or kind of obstructions in front of the moon, what type of month you would have. Near the end of 1941, I had seen a new moon in the Philippine Islands, but I had seen only a tip of it behind trees and clouds. And I thought, *Oh darn, I'm gonna have a bad month.*

Then on December 7th, the Japs hit Pearl Harbor, and eight hours later, the Philippine Islands. I was in the middle of World War II. I did not see the moon, in full view again, until the end of July 1945. When I looked up this time, there it was—as clear and as open in full view as I had ever seen it.

When I went back into the barracks, I told everyone that within 30 days we would be dead or free. It would be over. The guys looked at me as if I was crazy, and said, "Frazier—you of all people making a statement like that? You've *never* said anything like that. Why are you saying something like that now?" I replied, "I've seen a sign right from Heaven, and it's real. I don't understand it, but that is what will happen."

I thought again about what Howard Leachman had told me in the Philippines on the Tayabas Road detail. It gave me hope to remember that he had said that I would be the only one he knew who would make it back to the USA. I had no idea as to how that would happen, because it looked as though an invasion of Japan would be the only hope of ending the war. I couldn't think of any way that we POWs could survive an invasion. The Navy dive bombers were coming in almost every day. Many times we would see B-29s fly over, and a couple times a day, a reconnaissance plane would also fly over. The Japanese guards and workers were becoming more hostile. They were even training the old men, women, and children how to defend the homeland in case the Allied Forces invaded Japan.

Yet our interpreter became friendlier. The Japs weren't watching him as closely; it was reaching the point where they were more concerned about their own safety than about us. And now, our B-29s and dive bombers were flying in, yet no Jap planes could be seen defending the place. I am not sure if it was that way all over Japan, but it was true of the place where we were.

After they had moved us out to the old brick kiln, we had felt a little more secure, because the building was out in the open. Yet the guards were now yelling at us more and waking us up at night for no good reason. They told us if the B-29s came, we would have to move out into the rice field. I think they wanted to get out of the building themselves. While they guarded us, we did feel a bit safer from the general population, but we had our own plan of defense if the Japs tried anything.

Also, in the meantime, one of the men in our group had found a newspaper showing a picture of Okinawa and told us that it had looked like a battle picture. We understood then where all the Navy bombers were coming from. We knew if the Americans were that close, our aircraft carriers would also be close enough to send bombers over us. We figured that after the Navy pilot had seen us waving on the hill, the planes would target the ships and railroad cars. So we tried to stay away from the buildings in the dock area.

Within a few days, we noticed that all the Japs were exceptionally upset. Things were not as usual, and the interpreter came by to tell us that the United States had dropped a bomb so big, so powerful, that it had destroyed an entire large city. He said that even those people who had been 75 miles away from where the bomb had dropped were petrified.

At first, this sounded like a propaganda stunt they were pulling. But then, as we continued to take notice, we realized the Japs were acting differently. They were quiet, and they confined us to the inside of the brick kiln building. A few more guards came to watch us. We knew to stay quiet and keep a low profile.

The next morning, we were awakened by the guards yelling. They seemed to be extra hyper and very nervous. We were lined up, but not in the same way as if we were going to work. Instead, the guards marched us out to the edge of town to an open rice field. Soon a couple of trucks arrived. One was loaded with several new guards, and four were holding machine guns. The other trucks were loaded with picks and shovels on the back.

As they unloaded the trucks, it was absolutely nerve-racking to stand still and wait to see what was up. But by this time, we all had learned to keep our cool until we knew for sure what was happening.

But in all our minds, there was no doubt—this was where it was going to end. We were here to be executed and buried.

When all the guards were unloaded, the four with machine guns went to stand at each of the four corners of the rice field. We tried with all our might to keep each other calmed down. The guard in charge told us that we would be killed if the Allied Forces landed on the Japanese mainland. He warned us against trying to escape. We were there to dig our own graves.

I couldn't believe it. I was going to be buried in Japan. Somehow, we just had to get out of this! We didn't think that the Allied Forces were ready yet to invade, and that gave us some hope. We figured there might even be a few days to think about what we could do. Meanwhile, at this minute, I thought that if they were going to wait to kill me until I got my own grave dug, I would be the slowest grave digger on record.

We started digging—digging slowly. There was a heaviness in the air. It was quiet—so quiet, and we talked to each other in very low tones. We had learned how to be masters of the art of being slow, and also how to look like we were digging with the backs of our shovels. Time moved ever so slowly as well. When noon came, we were instructed to leave our tools and go back to camp. We would then return after the noon break.

While we were back in camp, we soldiers immediately discussed our next plan of action. We each teamed up with two others. We knew for certain they were going to shoot us, and when they started shooting, we all would break loose with our picks and shovels, running as fast as we could towards the guards with the machine guns, in hopes of killing some of the Japs. If any of us were able to get away, a group of three men would be the best number to go into hiding. Two could rest while the other one watched. This way, maybe some of us could survive and reach the American forces.

With this plan in place, we all were sent back to the rice field. We continued to make the digging look as hard as possible, and a few guys were slapped around a bit for not digging enough. I guess I must have dug about six inches that first day. At the end of the day, we were able to return to our barracks again.

That night many of the guys came close to losing control of their emotions. For the most part it was quiet, but every once in a while you could hear someone crying softly. It was difficult to believe that we had made it this far, only to die right before possibly being rescued. But this was no time to make any mistakes. If the guards started shooting for any reason, they would probably let loose and try to kill all of us...but the Japs would have their hands full. I considered this group of 340 POWs to be as tough as they come. They had been through three and a half years of slave labor, taken everything these Japs could dish out, and still they were standing face to face with their enemy. I, myself, had gotten my weight up to 165 pounds and was used to carrying over 100 lbs. on my back for hours at a time. It would be hard for ten Japs with just four machine guns to handle all of us.

During the night, we continued to tell each other how we felt about one other, giving comfort to the ones who needed help and reassurance that somehow this would work out. And if not, our plight would finally be over. All the pain, all the suffering—all of it would be done.

We would dig for another whole day, and then the third day came. As we fell out to work, the Japs seemed to handle us a little more carefully. The look on each of our faces was stern as we faced those machine guns. We never showed once that we were afraid of them.

Maybe this is the feeling that comes over brave men when the going gets tough and the pressure is at its highest. Even on this third day, our graves were still shallow. We didn't know how deep they had to be dug before the guards would start to shoot, and we didn't know what their orders were. So it was stand brave, face the enemy, no fear...no sign of fear. And still, we continued to dig.

At noon, the head guard told us once again that we would be returning to the brick kiln. A look of relief spread across every man's face.

As we walked back down the road to camp, I experienced a glimmer of hope. I never would have believed it, but here I was thanking God for another day of being a slave under these savage Japs. I had just experienced the highest level of tension—brought to the point of death—and then was given a temporary reprieve. I was literally weak in my knees. Marching between my close, dear friends was a true comfort. I couldn't think about going home; I didn't hope this was the end. At that moment, I was just grateful to be amongst my friends.

Each one of us hated to think about going back to the rice field after our lunch break. Surely, we had only hours before the end. I decided that at the sound of the first shot, I was going as fast as I could toward the closest guard with a machine gun and wrestle it away from him. Then I would not only kill the other guards, but I would go into the streets and shoot the kids who had spit, kicked, and even tried to urinate on us. ... It was now time to go.

We were ordered to fall out. And while standing there, all of a sudden...the air raid warning started! And it didn't take long before the short alarms sounded, which meant that the planes were in our area. We were already standing outside the building where we could see if any planes were coming. I felt a flare of anger come over me. *Come on B-29s! Drop one of those big bombs on these Japs and kill them all! I would be proud to die by our bombs instead of their bullets.*

But as we continued to look, we saw only one B-29 flying about 20,000 feet high. It was circling around the valley as if it was searching for something. Soon it started straight toward us. One of the 200 Coast Artillery guys yelled that the bomb bay door was open and that the plane was coming right in on us! There was nowhere to go, so we just fell flat on the ground and braced for the bomb that would hit us. Next, someone yelled that the bomb had come out!

Seconds later, we heard the shrill noise that we had heard so many times before. The ground shook as the bomb blasted through the big building across the street. The debris rained down on us— pieces of wood, shingles, dust, and dirt. I think every man yelled with relief and jumped with joy at the destruction of the building instead of our fragile lives. As the emergency equipment and personnel rushed to the building, we also helped remove the dead and wounded, and clean up the debris until 9:00 pm that evening.

What a wondrous transformation in just a few, mere moments! At lunch, we were having our last meal, because we knew...we knew the Japanese would be executing us that afternoon. Instead, we witnessed a miracle and were told the next morning that we would not be returning to the rice field to dig our own graves.

The guards were helping next door. Over 400 Japanese workers lie dead in the debris. The 2000-pound bomb had hit the building exactly where the big smokestack came out of the top—dead center. It took well over a day to clear the rubbish from the street. The interpreter came the next morning to tell us that the Japanese Emperor would be addressing the nation. He said that the Japanese and Americans had been in negotiations, and in the meantime, the bombing would stop.

12

NO ONE CAN MAKE ME STAY NOW

The Emperor spoke for two and a half hours, and we listened via loudspeakers that had been set up on the streets. One of the POW Marines, who had spent time in China and who once had a Japanese girlfriend, could understand most of the speech. So he interpreted for the rest of us. The Emperor explained to the Japanese people that the Allied Forces were preparing to invade the mainland, and when that happened, many of them would be killed. It was time to stop the war and time for all civilian and military personnel to lay down their arms.

Our guards, including the "Emperor" and "Sir Baloney Bird" had already moved out of our building and were posted outside the fence next to the road. We could also see other Japanese soldiers making their way up the mountain west of us, carrying guns and supplies. We had no idea where they were going.

Soon the interpreter came to tell us that an agreement of surrender had been approved and to let us know what we could expect. "You will be returned to the USA, and the guards who are now coming are here to protect you from any Japanese who might want to harm you," he assured us. *To protect us?!* **Protect...us?** I stood there with tears of joy running down my face. I couldn't believe it. I just couldn't believe it. Only a few days earlier, we had been digging our own graves—down to our last hope…but now, *now we were going home! Going home!* I looked around at all the faces and saw the same disbelief, shock, and surprise. I never, ever expected it to end this way, but oh my, what a blessing! I think it took two more days to sink in that are dreams, our impossible dreams, were coming true.

The interpreter continued to speak with us, and eventually asked if we would help him, his wife, and his children by signing a statement saying that he had been fair to us. Our captain, the ranking officer, agreed to prepare a letter for him, and every one of us had no problem signing it. The captain's gesture was somewhat surprising, especially since he and his lieutenant had done very little to help our own men during our imprisonment and in some cases caused a number of men to receive beatings from which they never recovered.

What most of us wanted to do was grab the guards—the Emperor, Sir Baloney Bird, along with about five others—drag them to the brick kiln, cast them into the large oven, and burn them to death! But…they were gone. All of them. Disappeared.

Someone brought us some red, white, and blue cloth, and we were instructed to make a simulation of our American flag and attach it to the top of the building. We were told to also display the number of men in the camp so the American reconnaissance planes could see it and then airdrop the appropriate amount of food, medicine, and clothes.

Food…clean clothes…maybe a pair of shoes without holes in them…and medicine for the sick! It was so hard to believe! Most of us were in shock. Even so, we couldn't get the flag made fast enough. And immediately, there was always someone outside looking for a sign of the plane.

The very next day, someone did spot a high-flying plane. We all ran out waving and jumping up and down, yelling as if they could hear us. We just had to laugh. It did us all good to be able to act kind of crazy and helped us realize even more that this wasn't just a dream anymore. It was for real! No one could sleep. We were running on pure adrenaline. Everyone was wishing for his favorite food and telling someone else how he wanted his steak cooked. We were all walking around and talking to each other about our homes and what we were going to do when we got there. I wondered if my girlfriend, Jamie, was still single and if she would want to see me. I also wondered how I was going to mend the hurt I had surely caused my family when I had left on July 3, 1941, without telling them where I was going. It was now August 1945. I hadn't seen them for more than four years, and sent only that one letter in November 1941, letting them know that I was in the Philippine Islands. I also wondered how Nelda was doing and if her family had made it through the war. I didn't know how to reach them now, and I figured that I wouldn't be going back to the Philippines before I went home. But then again, I had no idea what the Army planned to do with us.

A few days later, we finally saw a B-29 flying low across the valley. We also noticed that the new guards in the street were holding back a large Japanese crowd who had started forming around our building. As the B-29 made a couple of passes over us, we began to yell and wave. We noticed that the guards were also keeping the Japs away from a rice field just beyond our building, so we thought that maybe the drop might be there. When the plane made the next pass, we all saw that the bomb bay doors were open, and we were yelling, "This is it!"

As the 55-gallon drums, which had been welded together, came out of the bomb bay, the Japs in the street ran for their lives. Many of them thought they were actually being bombed! In fact, there was a stampede, and several were hurt as a result. They did not wait to notice that parachutes were opening instead. The drum with medicine went through the roof into the hospital area, while other drums were dropped into the rice field and sank into the ground. A few Japanese, who had stuck around, were able to get past the guards and ran for the drums along with us POWs. *Are you kidding me?! No way!* We knocked them down and sent them packing. Boy, did it feel good to hit a Jap without retribution.

We opened the drums as quickly as we could. Unbelievably, after all we had suffered and endured, and now even in the midst of this joyful experience, the captain started reciting regulations and began to choose certain men to help him take control. But even he could not put a damper on our celebration. This was our first American meal, which had been dropped like a gift from Heaven! Everyone was overwhelmed. I've never seen any group of little kids opening Christmas presents with as much excitement as we were opening those drums. You would have thought our new clothes and shoes were expensive, tailor-made items. We had to restrain ourselves to keep from eating too much. Surely, we wouldn't appreciate any other meal as much as we loved this first one. We would never have to eat soggy rice with black-eye worms again.

At different times during the day and night, many men took advantage of being able to go in and out of the brick kiln…but not me. For most of the time, I stayed inside. I had seen the Japanese retreating up the side of a mountain…with their guns and equipment. I didn't trust that they would do what the Emperor had told them to do and figured that they might be back to take revenge. I thought it best not to let my guard down. In fact, I told myself that this nightmare would not really be over until I set foot on the good old USA. Only then would I allow myself to relax a bit. There had been too many promises broken since April 1942 to trust anyone.

In the meantime, our captain and his lieutenant, who had appointed themselves as commanding chiefs, continued to bark orders. The captain insisted that he had been given secret orders from General MacArthur and that as soon as the bombing had stopped, he was to take charge. These two proceeded to appoint several of their favorites to higher ranks and gave them orders to begin telling everyone that close order drill would start and that all of us had to fall out the next morning at 7 a.m. Just looking around at the men's physical condition, and knowing firsthand what each of us had suffered for years now, you would have thought any respectable leader would have granted us just a little time to rest without being told what to do. It was unimaginable that one of our own officers could continue to treat us in this manner. Most of us had lost all respect for the captain and lieutenant long before now. Even so, we were up and fell out at 7 a.m. And the days passed slowly between August 15 and September 2, 1945—the day the official surrender was signed.

We wasted no time. On September 3rd, there was a movement to leave the camp, and a total of 21 men were ready to walk out dressed in our new khaki uniforms. We were determined to get as many of the sick out of there as quickly as possible in order to get medical help. Our plan was to board the train to Tokyo where we hoped to meet the Americans. I had gone to see Ralph, Roger, Mack, and Clyde to ask them if they were coming along. Mack said he was coming for sure. Ralph and Roger said they thought they would wait to be liberated. And when I asked Clyde what he was going to do, without hesitation he said, "You saved me once, and you're not going without me now."

All of us were getting ready to leave when the "captain's men" came to tell us that we would not be allowed to leave. None of us had been impressed with the captain's phony tale about the "secret orders from General MacArthur," and we weren't about to listen now. Some of the men even questioned the captain to his face, and he assured us that he was aware of every man's service number and insisted that if anyone left without his approval, they would face a court martial when they returned to the States. I wasn't impressed. I knew he did not have my service number, because I had never given it to anyone, most certainly not him, since my capture.

My standing Army orders were clear. If I was captured and then escaped or was released, I was to return to my unit as quickly as possible. Now, each man was expected to take care of himself, clean his bunk, assist with preparing the food, if needed, and help the sick. But after four years of war and slave labor, there was a limit as to what we'd take. The lieutenant tried to shove his weight around also, but we were not in the mood to listen to either one of them.

The early train was to arrive about 7:30 in the morning. So the 21 of us continued to line up, and we started towards the gate, with a few of the guys in the front carrying sticks. When some of the captain's guys stepped in front of us to stop us, we all yelled for them to get out of the way. We kept marching, pushing them aside.

As we passed the Japanese guard posted just outside the gate, he asked where we were going. The Navy man who spoke fluent Japanese replied, "Tokyo." The guard simply stepped aside. Then as we continued to walk towards the train station, the captain and his men followed us and yelled at the next Jap on duty at the train to stop us from boarding. But when we said we were on our way to Tokyo, this guard also stepped aside, and we hopped on the train.

Still not giving up, the captain's men came to the train and then tried to pull us off. As they got to the train door, the train started slowly pulling out. Those of us at the door just kicked them back. The Japanese men and women on the train thought it humorous, and yelled along with us at the ones who were staying. When we moved on down the track, we hung out the side and waved goodbye.

We all stayed close together. After three years, we knew how to handle ourselves with the Japanese. Most of us wanted revenge and had built up a hatred for them, but this was no time to be anything but polite and friendly. All went well, and most of us even got a little sleep.

When the train arrived in the Nagoya Terminal, we were told how to catch the next train to Tokyo. My thoughts were bouncing everywhere. It was hard to believe that we were traveling—for the first time in over three years, I was freely deciding where I wanted to go and on my way to meet the Americans and then get out of this country! During all the time that I had been a prisoner in Japan, I could not once visualize leaving Japan on a ship. And because I just couldn't bring myself to imagine that, I felt that I was probably not going to ever leave and instead lay down my life in this land. I said a short, quick prayer for God to take care of me and the other 20 men. He had pulled me through so many horrible times, and He would surely help us on this last stretch.

As we boarded the next train, we saw that it was full of Japanese soldiers along with a few women and children...and we felt less secure. *Had these guys just come in from battle? Would they take their anger out on us?* Every one of us realized that we had to stay quiet and keep a low profile. We each began to look for a seat when a Jap sergeant came to us and told us to follow him. As we followed him back several cars, we noticed that we weren't receiving very friendly looks. We even spoke to some of the Jap soldiers, but there was no response.

As we approached the last car on the train, we saw that it was a special car. We proceeded through a glass door and glanced about at the interior decorated in red with gold trim. A Japanese general sat at a desk located at the very back of the car and motioned for us to come closer. He then greeted us in English and made mention that he was the third-ranking general in the Japanese army, in charge of China, and was on his way to see General Togo. He asked where we had been imprisoned and where we were going. When we told him we were on our way to General MacArthur's headquarters, he informed us that General MacArthur was not in Tokyo, but in Hiroshima. None of us believed him, and decided to go on into downtown Tokyo.

Tokyo was totally, completely burned out. Very few buildings were standing. The B-29s had done their work. We also noticed that there were no Americans in sight, so we assumed we just needed to search around a little more. When we saw a streetcar not far away, we walked to that location and waited until the next one came. One of the guys told the next operator we had need of the streetcar so we could look for Americans, which meant that the conductor first remove all the Japanese people from the car so that we could board. The passengers complained, but the operator complied.

We rode that streetcar all over the place, but no one knew where the American troops were. After about two hours, we came upon a Jap army barracks, and thanking the conductor, we got off. As we walked up to the barracks, a guard came to attention and bowed to us. He must have thought we were operational troops. Our Navy chief told him there was no need for him to bow—no one had done that for three years. A surprised look came on his face, and then he asked where we were coming from.

When the chief told him we were POWs, he started begging us not to harm him. That was odd…he was the one holding the gun. He proceeded to call out for other Japanese troops, and about 25 came out of the building. A first lieutenant was the ranking officer. They likewise asked us not to harm them. Our chief gave his word, then told them we wanted to go to the American zone and asked if they would take us. The lieutenant agreed. We lined up in columns of two, then marched off to the train station with about 25 armed Jap soldiers around us. We had already traveled about 500 miles with no one to defend us; now 25 Japs were protecting us from all harm!

When we arrived at the train station about two miles down the road, the lieutenant jumped on board a car and ordered all the Japanese to disembark. They moved out. We loaded, and the train took us about ten miles and then stopped. The lieutenant told us that at this stop was an American zone where Japanese soldiers were not permitted. We thanked them as they all lined up and bowed to us.

When we got off the train, we looked around the station, but still did not see any Americans. Out in the street in front of us, though, many G.I. trucks were passing by. So we walked on out of the station and immediately saw an American soldier who was leaning up against a pole with a cigarette in his mouth and his gun hanging down western style. We noticed an 11th Airborne patch on his shirt. When we asked where General MacArthur's headquarters were, he said, "Don't ask me—I just got here at 3 a.m. this morning."

So we went on down the street and next tried to stop a truck, but with no luck. No one would give us a ride. We then walked to a small hill, and looking further down the road, we noticed two other parked G.I. trucks, one with the hood up. So we thought we'd try our luck with these guys. As we approached the trucks, a gray-haired master sergeant stepped forward and asked us where our truck was. When we told him we did not have one—that we were POWs—he almost fainted. I guess no one figured that a bunch of POWs would have the stamina or the guts to cross this many miles and take the initiative to find their own way out.

We asked him if he could direct us towards General MacArthur's headquarters, and he pointed down toward the bay, "See that tall building? That's where the headquarters are." Then he asked how we were going to get there.

"I'll guess we'll walk," someone said.

"Well…get in that truck, and I'll take you!"

As we pulled up in front of the headquarters building, we saw guards shoulder to shoulder around the place. An MP sergeant immediately appeared, and we told him who we were. He asked us to please wait right where we stood. Soon he returned with a major. We were finally in the hands of our own country! The feeling made my knees weak—to think that at last we were back under American protection.

As we approached the Grand Hotel, where General MacArthur's headquarters were located, we could see Old Glory flying in the breeze. Old Glory. I was overcome as I thought about the day on Battan in 1942 when we had buried that flag. On that day, we had every intention of someday returning to retrieve her. It was hard to comprehend how many lives—how many thousands and thousands of men had served and died during and after the surrender of Bataan and would never see Old Glory fly again. But here I was…I was still standing…I was a free man! Thank You, God!

The major had so many questions. One matter we had to explain was the issue regarding why the other POWs at Tsuraga hadn't come with us. After hearing about our experience, the major said that he hoped all the prisoners remained under appropriate care and that no one had died before the rest could be liberated. If there were any loss of life, he said that the captain could possibly be in some trouble. We were asked to sign a statement saying that we had made the trip without any difficulty and that we did not have access to any guns or other devices to protect us. At one point, the major asked how many men were in our group. One of the Marines among us promptly stepped out front, came to attention, shouted Japanese army orders, and we proceeded to dress and count off in Japanese…

"Lti (ichi)…ni…san…shi…go…roku…nana…hati (hachi)… kyu…jyu…jyu ichi…jyu ni…jyu san…jyu shi…jyu go…jyu roku…jyu nana…jyu hachi…jyu kyu…ni jyu…ni jyu ichi."

Then the Marine turned to the major and said, "All present and accounted for, Sir."

The major replied, "Take the men inside."

As we were escorted into the Grand Hotel, a crowd started to gather around us. We were given C rations, and simply shrank to a circle on the floor and proceeded to enjoy eating all we wanted. Eventually a lieutenant colonel came up to us and introduced himself as General MacArthur's liaison officer. He explained that the General was not able to come and greet us in person, but that we would not have any work to do and would be going home soon, and …WELCOME BACK!

One of the men spoke up and said, "That's okay…nobody wanted to see *him* anyway." Most everyone in the crowd turned their heads to laugh. The colonel found it necessary to leave as fast as he could.

Soon the major returned to tell us that we all checked out to be Americans, and he also welcomed us back. Then we were taken to another building where we changed into other clothes and shoes, and were sprayed with some kind of chemical for bugs. After that, we moved on to the next building where it was to be further determined if we needed any immediate medical help. As we walked from one building to the next, one of the men in our group couldn't help but to gawk at the nurses standing and waving at us from the deck of a ship. He wasn't paying attention to where he was going and walked right into the back of a truck…and his nose began to bleed. Another one of the men, likewise, while staring upward, was just one step away from walking off into the water. Mack had to grab him to keep him from falling in!

We proceeded into the building where a group of nurses and doctors were waiting to examine us. I was sitting there enjoying the attention of the nurse who was checking my heartbeat, temperature, and blood pressure. As she continued to hold my hand, she said, "Are you all right?"

I said, "Yes—I'm free at last."

She said, "Well, your pulse is going faster than at first."

I continued to gaze at her and said, "Look, it's been about four years since I've seen an American woman, and you *are* holding my hand."

She immediately jumped up, dropped my hand, and said to the doctor, "This man is ready for San Francisco!"

Then once again, our clothes were exchanged for another set. I didn't care how many times they wanted us to change clothes!

Before we went for our final checkup at the hospital ship docked close by, each of us was debriefed and asked about our treatment at the hands of the Japs—if we had been beaten or tortured. Our testimonies would be used as part of the war crimes courts, which would take place later. And we also gave reports of any Americans who had collaborated with the Japs and who had caused us harm by doing so. After this debriefing, it was determined that none of us would need additional help from the hospital ship crew.

So we were then escorted to a minesweeper ship docked in the bay for a wonderful, Navy-cooked meal. All the sailors were so interested in meeting us and asked us questions non-stop. We received a fabulous welcome home from everyone. When it came time for us to get some rest, we were directed to the beds, but... none of us could sleep. We were up and down for the next few hours, and then at 3 a.m. we were served a fine breakfast and then taken on to the airport for a flight to Okinawa.

We boarded a large cargo plane with no seats and were strapped to the side of the plane next to the windows. As we took off, we stared out at the valley below. Tokyo was dark. To the northwest was Mount Fuji. The tip of its peak was white, illuminated by the rising sun. Below the white an orange color was cast, which was bordered even further below by the darkness. As I continued to look out the window, I remembered again, interestingly, that I could never bring myself to think of leaving Japan on a ship. Indeed, I was now leaving on a plane. I was anxious to be on my way and to never return again.

As we flew over Okinawa Island, it looked as if every inch of land was covered with trucks, tanks, and equipment of all kinds. Ships filled the sea, and planes were flying in every direction. When we landed, a soldier was waiting at the foot of the gangplank with a warm welcome. He had already been informed that we had been POWs. I told that soldier that if they would outfit me immediately with enough of this equipment, I would go back to the mainland just one more time and kill every one of them.

We had no idea what to expect next, and to our surprise they loaded us on B-24s, with ten to each plane, and assigned us special places to sit. My seat was the tail gun blister. The crew consisted of a pilot, copilot, and navigator. They told us we had a job to do—we were to keep looking out for Jap planes, because a few had not given up yet. If we saw one, we were to yell out the location and they would give us the order to shoot if necessary.

But…the trip was uneventful. At one point, the pilot and copilot were even walking around the plane. So we asked who was flying the darn thing. They replied, "Two of *your* guys are sitting in our seats." We all yelled! The plane was miraculously flying on automatic pilot. At times, it would sway from side to side, causing the tail blister to go round and round. And then I would yell out, "Will someone come and lock this thing in place?" And everyone would holler and laugh. It was good to laugh.

When we came close to Nichols Field in the Philippines, the captain was ordered to move into a pattern and wait for instructions to land. We were running low on fuel, so the pilot yelled back at the air traffic controller that his gas was too low to circle that long. As they talked back and forth, the captain eventually said, "I don't care what you want me to do. I've got to land. I'm coming in…."

As we went in low, the plane hit the ground hard, bounced clear up above the buildings, then came down hard again. We held on for dear life! We rolled down the runway and were listing to the right. When we finally got off that plane, we could see that the landing gear on the right side had been bent. What an arrival!

Two days ago, we had walked out of a Japanese prison camp, and now we were in the Philippines! We were immediately taken to a barracks that had already been used to clear POWs who had been released when MacArthur had returned to the Philippines several months before. I wasted no time in finding Western Union and sending a telegram to my folks, even though a major in Tokyo had already told us that our families would be notified that we were safe. To make sure that my family would understand that it was really me sending the message, I used my middle name, Dowling.

The next morning I was asked to come to the orderly room. When I walked into the room, there was Nelda's brother, whom she had called "Buddy"—the one who had given me the hunting knife that I used to kill the Jap who had attacked me with a bayonet at the Battle of the Points. He had been hoping that I would still be alive, and was watching and waiting for me to return to the Philippines. Without hesitation, he grabbed and hugged me. When I moved back to look at him, I saw that he had tears in his eyes. He had a hard time telling me that Nelda had been killed in 1944 during an attack by the Japanese on their camp. He wanted me to put off going on to the USA and instead stay with his family for a while.

Even though I was very saddened by the news about Nelda, I could not miss the chance to get on home as quickly as possible. Buddy made sure that I knew I was welcome to stay with them at any time and asked me to please come back to the islands some-day. Until that time, we agreed to keep in touch. He then handed me the very knife that he had made and given to me three years earlier—the knife that Nelda had carried out of Bataan. It still had Japanese blood on the leather of the handle. I was honored that he had thought to give it to me. As he walked away, he couldn't hold back the tears.

A typhoon was heading into the islands, so all planes going to the States had been grounded. We had a choice. We could wait until the typhoon had passed…or take a ship out within a couple of days. I talked to Clyde and Mack—we decided on the ship, the troop transport *USS Pope*.

13

THE UNITED STATES OF AMERICA!

As we climbed onto the trucks that would take us to board the *USS Pope*, my thoughts were mixed about leaving the Philippines. I was very happy...for sure...but my emotions were in a turmoil. I was thinking about Howard Leachman...Turesky...Lucas...Engram ...Sergeant Warren...Nelda...Vargas...and so many others who had touched my life during this terrible ordeal. My heart was full of tenderness for the Filipino people who had lent a hand to me. And I was overflowing with the deepest respect for the many brave and heroic men who had given their all. I would always admire and remember each one of them.

There was an unbreakable bond that would hold me to these people who were not here to share the happiness that I was just ahead of me. So many times I've continued to ask myself, "Why me?" How did Howard know that I would be the only one he knew who would experience this moment of freedom? It was like I had walked through a large, endless minefield with an angel safely guiding me each step of the way.

It was September 8, 1945. How totally different this trip to the pier was from the one three years earlier, in 1942, when we were loaded onto a Japanese freighter as slaves and shipped away to a prison in Japan. Now, when I arrived at the pier, I looked back towards the Old Walled City with uncertain thoughts about the future. I wondered if I could handle being a free man again. With every step I took up that gangplank, I longed to put the past behind me. Little did I realize that the past would remain with me forever.

I noticed that truckloads of GIs were pulling up to the pier, and these soldiers were jumping off and also reloading onto the ship. I thought surely they couldn't all be POWs. I soon found out that most of these men had fought their way from Australia in some of the most horrid battles of the war. I was proud to be returning to the United States of America with such valiant men. Most of them had been fighting since 1942, and their cruel experiences were reflected in their tired and worn faces. Some were hard and cold inside. I understood that they had also walked through the gates of hell and came out the other side. The ones who were able to talk expressed what this trip home meant to them—it was the same for all of us.

As we sailed out of Manila Bay, I glanced to the right—there was Bataan; and then I glanced to the left—there was Corregidor. There was an emptiness inside. Clyde had tears in his eyes, as did I. We didn't say a word…we didn't have to.

We were told it would take about 16 days to reach San Francisco—16 days without any assigned duty. But most of the POWs were looking for something to do anyway. The first day they opened the ship PX, I used some of my small advance pay, which I had received in the Philippines, to buy a box of 24 Baby Ruth bars. Once I tasted the first one, I knew they wouldn't last long. Before the night was over, I had eaten every one of them.

The ship's chief cook and I got to know each other pretty well too. He asked me what food I had missed the most, and I told him, "Potato salad and ice cream." "Well," he said, "I can't get my hands on any salad, but I'll be right back with the ice cream. Just wait, right here." When he came back a few minutes later, he was carrying a Navy pitcher full of various flavors of ice cream, along with a *big* spoon.

I sat myself down under a stairway and started to eat away. Every so often, the cook came by to ask how I was doing. Before long, I handed back the pitcher to him. He looked in it and said, "Man, you ate it all—nearly a gallon!" On that trip across the Pacific, I ate all I could eat and still got up from the table hungry. I could feel the weight stacking up on me. When I had left Japan, I weighed about 168 pounds. Now, already, I could barely button my pants, and my shirt buttons were about to pop. A few times, I went up on deck to attempt to do some exercises, but there was no stopping the weight gain.

The 16 days passed slowly, and it seemed more like a month before we finally approached the West Coast. Every man aboard was getting excited, especially about sailing under the Golden Gate Bridge into the San Francisco Bay. Back home—USA! We were so wound up that many of us had even been discussing just what we would do when the bridge came into sight. To me, it would be like arriving at the heavenly Golden Gates. I knew I had officially regained my freedom the day I walked into General MacArthur's headquarters in Japan, but that feeling was nothing like this. My heart was pounding, and I'm sure my pulse was beating faster than when the nurse had held my hand in Japan.

September 24, 1945 in San Francisco was overcast with scattered clouds. Every spot on the deck was taken. I expected that when the bridge came into view, the men on the ship would act just like those of us who had stood on that knoll in Japan when the first dive bombers came in to bomb the docks. We all would be jumping and yelling, just like a bunch of crazy idiots at a good football game. Everyone was hoping to be the first to see it. All of a sudden, a soft, low voice said, "There it is…right ahead of us." I saw that we were only a short distance from the bridge, and I swallowed. No one said a word. Everyone looked at the bridge in total silence for several minutes. It was silent. Like a holy hush…

Then all hell broke loose! It's a wonder someone was not knocked overboard. You could not stand still or keep from yelling. It was the most special gift in the world! Home sweet home.

Every man aboard was anxiously getting his things together, ready to set foot on US soil. Even the men who had been quiet could now not stop yelling. The *USS Pope* went straight to its designated pier with no delay. As we approached the pier, we saw Old Glory waving in the breeze high above it. What a sight. My legs were weak, and my breath came in gasps.

After order was restored, the POWs were the first to disembark. I was the second one to leave the ship. As soon as I touched American soil, I stopped, got down on my knees, and kissed the ground. The guy ahead of me had turned and then also knelt down beside me. After that, most of the men followed suit.

A large crowd of people waited a short distance away, ready to welcome their loved ones home. They were waving American flags and shouting, "Welcome home!" What a feeling now to be walking on American soil—land that so many times I thought I would never see again. It was hard to believe, and a feeling of unreality pervaded everything. It was just about impossible to think it was happening!

As we loaded onto buses nearby, all of us were hugging each other. The joy we shared together was one of love and understanding that I will never forget—we meant so much to each other. No one was there to greet us POWs, but we weren't surprised or disappointed. I assumed that our families didn't yet know we were coming. It didn't matter—it was enough to share this time with each other.

From the pier, we were taken to Letterman General Hospital for a routine examination. We were assigned to stay at a building some distance from the main hospital, and we'd be taken care of by a nurse and a few aides. As we walked into the building, we saw *real* beds, up off the floor, made up nice and clean…one for each of us. No straw mats. And no lice.

As I walked over to choose a bed, I noticed a pitcher of water on a side table along with a few little tidbits to eat. This simple gesture of thoughtfulness was overwhelming. I was so grateful. At about 8 p.m. a very young nurse came on duty. She had recently graduated from nursing school, and this was her first day of work. She explained that bed check was at 9 p.m. and that everyone must be in bed at that time. Just before the lights were turned off, she came in to check on each of us one more time and to tell us that if we needed anything during the night, we could find her at the nurses' station. She reminded us all to be quiet and considerate of others.

About 30 minutes after the lights had been turned off, most of us were still having trouble falling to sleep in a soft bed. Soon some were on the floor with pillows and a blanket. The restroom was full of men, each one confessing that he just could not sleep. A few even went outside and crawled up next to the building. In time, the young nurse made her rounds back through the floor. When she saw that most of the beds were empty, she became alarmed and snapped on the lights. She then proceeded to fly around on the floor, into the restroom, back to the floor, urging the men to get back to their beds.

When she stopped a few seconds to take a count, she discovered there were still some men missing. So she went back to her station in frantic mode to call someone to report that several men were missing. When the head nurse arrived, the young nurse was already crying, saying she simply couldn't handle a bunch of military men who would not obey her orders.

The head nurse asked some of us where the other men could be found. We took her around to the back of the building and showed her where the missing men were sleeping. And they *were sleeping*—very comfortably. The head nurse turned to the rest of us and said, "Okay men, sleep wherever you want to." Most got on the floor. It took about five days before we were able to sleep restfully on clean, elaborate beds.

In August 1941, when I had been waiting at San Francisco to be shipped to the Philippines, I had decided to deposit ten dollars of my military pay each month to the Bank of America. So, when Clyde and I got a pass to go into the city, we went back to that bank and withdrew my money. Over four years later, I had saved $500 in my bank account. That night, we treated ourselves to Playland Beach, a park with roller coasters and lots of other rides. Clyde and I met two girls, and because we had had a few beers, we took them on the roller coaster with us about three times. After the rides, Clyde and I went to a restaurant, and at the end of the meal, the waitress presented us with a bill for two dollars. When I handed the pretty girl a twenty-dollar bill, Clyde grinned at her and smoothly said, "Just keep the change, Sweetie." He gave away my money!

A couple of days later, we were told we could make one long-distance phone call and talk as long as we wanted to at government expense. It was time for me to call home and let the family know that I was alive and well in San Francisco. As I dialed the number and the phone started to ring, I wondered what they would say and whether they would be angry with me. I wasn't sure just how to handle myself. After all, I had left without telling them where I was going and then hadn't sent word until I wrote that letter from the Philippines in November 1941. Now, nearly four years later, I was a little apprehensive. Perhaps they were really angry with me, especially for getting captured and imprisoned as a POW, just like Tokyo Rose had said they would be.

My mother answered the phone. I took a breath and said, "Hi, Mother. It's me—Dowling. And the phone went dead. I waited for a few seconds. Then my Aunt Ruby answered the phone by saying, "Who is this?"

Again, I said, "This is Dowling." The phone went dead again. I waited for a few more seconds, and soon my oldest sister, Sarah Nell, answered the phone. She likewise asked, "Who is this?" "Hi… it's Dowling." And, no joke, the phone went dead again.

I was still waiting when Dad came to the phone. By this time, he was irritated at what he assumed was a prank call. He asked in an angry authoritative voice, "Who is this!?"

"Dowling—it's me, Dad. It's Dowling," I repeated one more time.

"I knew you weren't dead. I knew you weren't dead." I could hear the certainty along with the pride in his voice. He then said, "But I think I have three women on my hands who look like they *are* dead."

He told me to hold on for just a moment. I couldn't help but to smile as he went and got a pitcher of water, and poured some in each of their faces. When he came back to the telephone, he said, "Well, it looks like they're still in the land of the living."

Dad asked where I was and a dozen other questions. He said that, yes, they had received a few telegrams from the Army. The first one was a message informing them that I was missing in action. Two and a half months later, they received a second telegram notifying them that the Army had no word that I was alive, and so assumed that I was dead. Then several months before I would arrive home, an Army representative came to see them. He was holding my dog tags and regretted to inform them that my remains had been found in the mass grave at Camp O'Donnell, the burial site where I had thrown them, in 1942.

The Army had tried to pay them $10,000 to settle my life in- surance claim. My Dad then asked if he would have to repay the money if I were later found alive. The representative said that, in that case, the Army would request repayment. So my Dad told them to just keep the money. He had a feeling that I was still alive. He also told them that if anyone could make it, he knew his son could. Then, my family had received the telegrams from the Army and from me, saying that I was alive and on my way home. Needless to say, they were almost afraid to believe that it could be true. Dad informed me that my brother Rupert was also in the service somewhere close to Japan and that my brother O'Vaughn was still in Europe, but was expected home anytime.

When my oldest sister, Sarah Nell, got back on the phone, she wanted to know if I was in bad shape and how long I would be staying at Letterman Hospital. If I would be there for a while, she said, some of the family would come to see me. I told them that I would be home soon, and each of them returned to the phone to express joy and thankfulness that I was alive. I felt relieved and so much better. In the meantime, I rested and enjoyed my stay at the hospital.

One day while we POWs were lounging around on the grass outside the hospital, a train brought five railroad cars into the area. The engine was unhooked from the cars and moved on, leaving the cars on the tracks nearby. Soon a crew came to unload the cars, which contained supplies for the hospital. At noontime, they closed the car doors and left for a lunch break.

The six of us must have been bored because we looked at each other with the same thought in mind. The tracks curved around a small hill, and it was time to have some fun. We ducked down and sprinted over to the cars, where we began to move them. We first unhooked the last car using a technique we had learned in Japan. One by one, we moved all the cars out of sight. When the crew came back to pick up where they head left off, we watched as they looked all around in confusion. Then we heard the sergeant in charge get on his phone to report that the train had come back and moved the cars out. He requested that someone call the railroad and tell them to bring the cars back. After a while, the sergeant received a call and was informed that the train had not come back to the hospital and had not moved any of the cars.

"Well, five cars didn't just vanish into thin air!" the sergeant declared.

In the meantime, no one thought to check and see if the cars had been moved on around the tracks. All this time we were having a good laugh. Soon a major arrived, and within a few minutes, he noticed us guys sitting there and asked, "How long have you guys been sitting there? You see where or how the cars were moved?"

"Yes, Sir," we answered. "They're around the turn in the tracks."

The sergeant took off and then came back to report that they were indeed where we said they were.

When the major asked us who had moved the cars, we could not keep from laughing. "This is a serious matter," he blustered. "If you guys know anything, you have to tell me."

We confessed and told him that we had moved them.

"You guys!?" he said, with a surprised look on his face. "How did you do that?"

We then explained how we had learned, as POWs in Japan, to move railroad cars.

After listening for a minute, he said, "Well…would you guys go and move them back for us?"

All of us, and all of them. went down around the tracks. They wanted to see us perform this "miracle." We put our shoulders against the first car and started pushing, using the Japanese words for push, "*Hey, no gosha!*" over and over again. As we gradually speeded up the pushes, the cars started to move. The guys watching could not believe their eyes. It took a little while, but we did get the cars back in place. While the major thought what we POWs had done was a very poor joke, he let the matter drop.

Everyone at Letterman General Hospital was good to us. Because they had previously treated many of the POWs from the

Philippines, they were aware of just what we needed. In the meantime, we all enjoyed our new freedom.

The psychological counseling we received was definitely to the point, and you could say it covered the basics. The doctor whose job it was to "repatriate" us was a no-nonsense kind of guy. His feeling was that if you could walk and talk, you were ready to face the world like a normal person. We listened to about 20 minutes of information like, "Everywhere you go to eat they will furnish knives, spoons, and forks. All restrooms have toilet paper. When asking for food to be passed to you, ask politely. Use the word, 'please.' " After those bits of advice, he abruptly said, "Now go out and act normal."

We would soon have a chance to try out our skills at acting normal. After seven days of treatment, we learned that the 21 of us would fly back East with a stop at the Phoenix, Arizona Air Force Base, then at Dallas, New Orleans, and Thomasville, Georgia. They would fly each one of us as close as possible to his hometown. As we flew about 15,000 feet over the Rocky Mountains in our DC-3, it was cold, and the cabin was not pressurized. Then when we dropped down to the Arizona desert where it was like an oven. I was anxious to get home.

When we landed at Phoenix, we were told that we were to be guests of honor that evening at a dance and would sit at the base commander's table. That afternoon, Clyde and I decided to take a walk down the street from the barracks where we were to spend the night. When we started to pass by this small building, a lady came out asking if we were with the POW group. She thought that it was likely because of the uniforms we were wearing; then she asked us to come in. While we were talking to this lady, I was looking out a window and noticed the two nurses, who had been traveling on our plane, walking by. I went out to say hello and asked if they would be attending the dance that night. They said they had not been invited to the commander's dance, so we invited them to come in with us.

The lady who ran this little recreation unit then called two other girls, asking them to come down to see us. Soon, three other girls showed up, and we were offered some drinks and beer. There was a jukebox, and someone suggested that we dance. When the music started, Clyde and I danced with a different girl every song. We paid no attention to time, and neither did the girls. When closing time came at 10 p.m., we were surprised to realize it was that late.

As the nurses were leaving, we asked them if they would play along in a little joke the next morning when we all boarded the plane. We wanted them to call us sweet names to make the other guys jealous, and the girls agreed. When we walked into the barracks later that night, the guys asked where we had been. They mentioned that the MPs had been looking for us and also for the commander's daughter. Apparently, they thought we had done something to her.

After we revealed where we had been to the sergeant in charge of the barracks, he called the MPs who promptly showed up, wanting to know if we had seen the missing daughter. We also told them where we had been and said that only the two nurses and the three girls who lived on the base had been with us at the recreational building. Calls were made to the commander's home and also to the lady who invited us into the building. Within 30 minutes it was all cleared up as far as the MPs were concerned, but...the other 19 POWs were ready to tear us apart. They had attended the dance with a couple thousand airmen and only 200 girls, while Clyde and I had the company of five of them all to ourselves.

The next morning as we boarded the plane, the nurses called Clyde and me "Darling" and kissed us on the cheeks. They really poured it on, making comments about how close we all were to each other, and so on. Boy, did that get the guys going again.

As we made our way toward our first drop off in Dallas, I felt a little sad about leaving the others…after all we had been through together. It was hard to say goodbye. After Dallas, it was New Orleans. That's where Mack and Clyde got off. Clyde and I had been especially close. We hugged goodbye with a promise to see each other later.

Now there were only six of us who were flying on to Thomasville, Georgia, to a small Army hospital 200 miles from my home. When I arrived, I called home and talked to my sister again. She asked the usual questions about my health and insisted that the family would come see me. There was no need for my family to make the trip. At that point I was gaining weight fast, and outside of my bad limp caused by the old bayonet wound, my health was as good as anyone could expect.

I was wondering about my girlfriend, but didn't have the nerve to ask. I assumed that no one in my family ever found out anything about what had happened between Jamie and me before I had joined the Army in 1941. And anyway, it was unlikely that she would have waited this long for me.

My sister continued to talk and say that they still hadn't heard from my brother O'Vaughn who was in Europe. They were becoming worried that something had happened to him at the War's end, and in the meantime could not find out anything from the Army. We agreed that there was nothing we could do but wait.

When the six of us POWs asked the doctor how long we would have to stay in Thomasville, he told us maybe a couple of weeks. I immediately let him know that I wanted to go home right away. He said, "Well, that'll be kind of hard to do because your clothes have been locked up." I looked him in the eyes and said, "Clothes? You can have my clothes. These pajamas are good enough, and I can leave wearing them."

He said, "Okay, son. If you want to go that bad, I'll see what I can do." The next morning when he made his rounds, he told me I could leave the next day on a 45-day leave. And boy, was I in high spirits. When I called my sister to let her know I was coming home, she was so excited. Her phone had rung just a few minutes earlier, and it was an operator who had said there was a collect call from Georgia. Sarah Nell thought it was me. So when she answered the phone, she called out my name. The voice on the other end of the line said, "No…this is O'Vaughn. Why did you say, 'Dowling'?"

"Oh, O'Vaughn…oh, it's you! I'm so glad it's you. You're not going to believe this…Dowling's alive! And he's in Thomasville, Georgia!"

Within a few minutes on the same day, my family discovered that O'Vaughn was alive, and O'Vaughn received the news that I was alive as well.

14

THE LAST LEG
OF A LONG JOURNEY

I was going home to Fort Deposit, Alabama. My ultimate dream was coming true—but a dream not without some apprehension.

I had been gone for more than four years—since the summer after my high school graduation. Four years—the same amount of time other high school graduates took to go off to a university and earn a college degree, or establish a career, or get married and start a family. As for me, I had been to hell and back, and had changed in almost every way. From what I could see, the whole United States had changed. What World War II had done to all of us was hard for me to understand.

Now I would have to face some of the problems left unresolved since July 1941. I assumed there would probably be a lot of hurt feelings between my family and me. Leaving like I did, without telling anyone, I might now find that some of my family wouldn't be able to forgive me, nor might they understand who I had become. Likewise, I might not understand them. I also wondered if my girlfriend, Jamie, was still around and whether or not she had gotten married. Would we have anything in common, except for the experiences we had shared so long ago? And would it be possible to pick up where we had left off?

I was already missing the close friendship and camaraderie of other POWs. They had become such an integral part of me, and I knew this closeness would never go away. When you live with someone, day after day, in as close proximity as we had—someone who truly will lay down his life for you—that bond becomes as close as your own blood. I always knew how they felt, and they knew how I felt.

Now that I was free, I found myself wondering if I could even accept the concept of freedom. Could I become a "normal" person again? No one back home could possibly relate to my years as a slave in a prison camp. They had lived through no experience even remotely comparable to it. Sometimes I had considered not even going back home. There was no doubt that there would be some difficult adjustment ahead. Moreover, the words of Tokyo Rose on the radio in Bataan had done some serious damage in my mind. I still wrestled with the thought that our country looked upon us as cowards and did not want us back. If that turned out to be true, I didn't know if I could handle that kind of treatment after I had already endured so much. But I did know that God had gotten me through a difficult time, and I had faith that He would help me now. I would surely need Him.

Getting home meant one more ride—a bus ride of several hours. When the doctor gave us POWs our release to go on leave, I immediately made a call to my cousin, Jerome Harrison, who lived closer to the hospital than my family had. I told him that I would be riding the bus to his town on October 9th, and asked him if he would then take me the rest of the way home. He said he would sure be happy to do so. I also wanted to have the chance to talk to him before meeting my family—to try to get some idea of what kind of reception I might expect when I arrived home.

It was so good to see him. I was genuinely amazed at his excitement about my being home after so long. His kindness was very special, and made me feel so much better. He had been told that soldiers who had gone through what I had, might be reluctant to talk about their experiences, and he was very careful about the questions he asked. On the other hand, I had no problem telling him anything he wanted to know. He and I had always been as close as cousins could be back in our school days. I did notice, however, that he too, had grown and changed while I had been gone. And he had definitely followed my suggestion to ride my motorcycle while I was gone. In fact, I later discovered he had worn it out!

As soon as we pulled up to the house, everyone—everyone ran out! They were grabbing me and hugging me and slobbering all over me. And to my surprise, my brother O'Vaughn was already there. He had arrived from Europe just a few hours earlier. My mother, father, oldest sister Sarah Nell, youngest sister Betty Carolyn, O'Vaughn's wife Mabel, and his daughter Vonciel—they were all there.

And as for my anxiety and concerns about whether or not I would be welcomed…well, they evaporated into thin air. The love that was expressed was beyond anything I could have imagined. Tears of joy were on most everyone's face. Sarah Nell had an especially hard time controlling herself. In fact, she was simply beside herself. She and I had always been close, and she just could not stop hugging me. She showed the same love she had always expressed to me, plus much more. Little Vonciel was so adorable and excited to have her daddy there—someone she had known only from looking at a picture.

My father had changed the least of anyone. With his sense of humor, he showed me that he was proud that I was back and was safe. And there was my mother…my mother. I guess only another mother can really relate to the heartache and pain a mother finds almost impossible to bear when she thinks of her very own child being captured, tortured, and possibly slain. I could tell that she had suffered much. She was quiet and in somewhat of a daze, but

I knew her heart was now simply bursting. And then there was my youngest sister. It's humorous how some people, once they think they have lost you forever, truly regret the way they had treated you. Betty Carolyn was just as excited as everyone else, and had to tell me immediately how sorry she was that as we were growing up, she would tell Mother that I had hit her when I hadn't, which would then cause me to get more than a few spankings.

Later, when my oldest brother Waverly came over with his family, he too said it was hard to believe that I was home safe. He had been trying to accept the fact that I was dead. His wife, Margaret, a school teacher, was very glad to see me home as well, but couldn't help to add, "You should never have gone in the first place."

Waverly and Margaret's oldest child, Johnny, said he thought I was never going to get back. When the US had entered the War, little Johnny had been recovering from an operation. They told me the story of how he had been listening to a radio while recuperating in bed and all of a sudden, he started to cry. When asked what was wrong, he said the Japanese had bombed the Philippine Islands and that's where his Uncle Dowling was stationed.

Their oldest daughter, Sarah Glenn, just stood back and stared. She kept looking at me as if to ask, "Who are you...and why is there so much fuss about you?" And their youngest child (at that time) was a pretty little girl named Thelma. She was just too young to understand all of what was going on with these Army guys.

The news that both O'Vaughn and I were coming home at the same time had already caused quite a stir in our small town. And as we made our way into the house and closed the door, people continued to pass by, honking their horns, while others continued to call, giving their best wishes and welcoming us home.

Soon, my mother and the other women prepared a big dinner for us. I was now sitting down at the table with my family eating the meal I had dreamed about so many times and that I was so sure would never come to pass. This was the greatest gift I could ever receive.

Between O'Vaughn and me, the war stories were going strong. Everyone else, likewise, had so many stories to share, especially about what the folks at home had to put up with—like the rationing of tires…gas…sugar…meat…stockings…and many other items that were in very short supply.

My father related a humorous story about getting tire ration coupons at the courthouse, and then Sarah Nell told about two young boys coming to her house selling magazines. Supposedly they were raising money for War Bonds. When she told them that she didn't believe she wanted any, they started ridiculing her, telling her that she was not a true American, had no interest in helping our boys overseas, and that she didn't understand what the War was all about. Well…that did it! And she set them straight. She told them that she had one brother in a POW camp somewhere in the Far East, and another brother in Europe who had been in the drive from Africa to Italy and beyond. Another brother was in the U.S. Navy in the Far East waiting for the invasion of Japan. So, they had better get out of there before she called the police!

My little sister Betty wanted me to know that our dog, Tan, had missed me so much. Being the youngest boy, I guess I had spent more time with him than anyone else had. Betty said that after the War had started, Tan began to howl at night. As he would howl, Mother would start to cry. The louder he howled, the more Mother would cry. Betty would have to bring him inside to calm him down.

After dinner my mother said she had a surprise for O'Vaughn and me, and she left the room. When she returned, she was carrying several packages and placed them on the coffee table. "Here are your Christmas gifts for each Christmas you missed," she told us. Then she added, "Wait…I have something else."

When she returned to the living room again, she was carrying the mirror/hat rack that had hung on the hallway wall at the farmhouse. Two hats were still hanging on it. One was the hat that

I had hung there when I rode off on my motorcycle, and the other one was O'Vaughn's that he had hung there the day he left for the Army. When my family had moved from the farm to town, my mother had carried along the mirror on her lap and said that no one was to take those two hats off until her boys returned home. Even after she received the news that I was presumed dead, she insisted that the hats stay in place. Those hats would be a continued ray of hope that her boys would someday make it back home. My father too never gave up—he always had a feeling that I was still alive and that I would manage somehow to come back. I took my hat off the rack—it had been damaged by some moths, scarred just like me, but nevertheless was home. My mother kept that hat until the house burned in 1949.

Our celebration went on into the wee hours of the night. There was so much to catch up on with both of us and with the rest of the family, we just couldn't bear to go to bed. It was early morning before we finally got any rest.

The next day O'Vaughn and I wanted to go up the street about half a block to Raymond Davis' store, to get a Coke, but mostly to visit with the people in town. We had just gotten to the curb of the street when car after car began to stop, passengers waving out the windows, welcoming us home, and just wanting to chat for a while. The cars kept coming by until 4 p.m., and someone else eventually went to get us that Coke. When we were able to get back to the house, the phone didn't stop ringing. That Sunday, we all went together to the Methodist church. My mother was beside herself. There's something so special, so meaningful sitting with your entire family, all together, at church. Everyone in attendance there extended an overwhelming love and welcomed us back home.

Almost everyone was so interested in knowing what had really happened to me in the POW camps. I was more than glad to answer their questions and satisfy their curiosity. Before long I had over a hundred invitations to come to dinner and talk about my experiences. I think it did me some good to talk everything out—it was somewhat of a purging experience. In the meantime, I also was eating everything in sight, but still getting up from the table feeling hungry and like I needed to eat more. My appetite stayed that way all through the winter and until the weather got warm in the spring.

The first few days home, I kept thinking about Jamie—if she was still in town and whether she had ever gotten married. I finally got the nerve to call a fellow classmate to ask about her. He said she had waited for me for over three years. When word came that I was dead, though, she had started her life over again. Then he said, "I hate to tell you this…but she's getting married this coming Sunday."

My heart dropped. But I couldn't blame her for not waiting on me. The only time I saw her again was about two months after her wedding. We said a few words to each other, and she finally just said, "I'm so sorry…please don't blame me." As I gazed at her, I still felt so close to her, and simply wished her the best of luck.

It took me a while to get over my feelings for her. So many times the hope that she was waiting for me gave me the needed strength to push myself…to keep going…and not give up. There were even times in the slave labor camps when my system was so low that I couldn't remember the names of some of my family, yet I could remember Jamie. I would never forget how I felt when she got on the train that morning of July 3, 1941.

After some special training at the U.S. Naval Station, Bainbridge, Maryland, my brother Rupert had headed to the South Pacific as a member of a military government team. Rupert joined the First Marine Division in February 1945, on the island of Pavuvu, located in the Russell Islands, a part of the Solomon Islands. He was now supposed to be in the Far East, but we were not given any confirmation that he was really there, so we had no idea exactly where he was.

The mission of a military government team was to follow the invading Forces into cleared enemy territory and locate and take care of the civilian population. The team would round up women, children, and the elderly; account for them; feed them; and treat their medical needs. Rupert did not know until his ship left Pavuvu that his next destination was Okinawa, the largest of the Ryukyu Islands, just 90 miles from Japan.

After the U.S. Forces landed on Okinawa on April 1, 1945, the military government team went ashore the next day. This battle was one of the fiercest of the Pacific during World War II, and there were many civilians who needed care in the aftermath.

Then, word came that there were considerable Japanese forces on Iheya Shima, a small island northwest of Okinawa, and an invasion was planned for May 1945. This invasion also required a government military team, and Rupert was selected as a member. The weather was terrible, and there were several postponements, but eventually Iheya Shima was invaded with little resistance. Once again, there were many civilians who needed the help of the government team.

Rupert had worked on Iheya Shima from May until August 1945, when the atomic bombs were dropped on Hiroshima and Nagasaki, bringing the War with Japan to a close. The last two kamikazi planes to leave Japan landed on Iheya Shima without causing any damage to our Forces.

Rupert knew that I had been sent from the Philippines to Japan as a prisoner of war. As soon as word was received that the War was over and the treaty was signed, Rupert received permission from his commanding officer to go to Okinawa to see if he could find out anything about the prisoners. He stayed on Okinawa for about ten days, but found nothing. At the request of his commanding officer, Rupert returned to Iheya Shima. Later, Rupert heard that I had been on Okinawa at the same time he was, on my way home, but he had not been able to locate me. I, of course, had no idea that

Rupert was even in that part of the world, or was even a member of the Armed Forces. Based on the point system for returning to the United States, Rupert was not able to return home until March 1946—five months after I had returned. Amazingly, there were three brothers in our family who served abroad in World War II and who came home safely. We were the fortunate ones.

During the time I was home on leave, I was notified that the Thomasville Army Hospital was closing and that I should now report to Moore General Hospital in North Carolina at the end of my 45 days. In the meantime, my younger sister Betty determined that it was time for her 20-year-old brother to meet some nice girls, and lined up about 15 ladies to go out with me. But I wasn't ready. I still wasn't over my feelings for Jamie, the girl I had loved so much. To me, a date was supposed to be fun, a time to become better acquainted, and a time to lay a foundation for a deeper friendship or a more mature relationship. I just wasn't interested.

When I reported to Moore General Army Hospital, the other five POWs who had traveled back across the USA with me were there too. They all had joyful stories and tales of wonderful reunions with their families.

The hospital had graciously assigned a location where we could stay together, and everyone there treated us with kindness and respect. It was now time to undergo the necessary examinations to determine if we were fit to stay in the Army. Even though the Army was in the process of downsizing, we could choose to remain in the service, if we passed the examinations, because we had already been regular Army before the War.

My thoughts were to first obtain a release from the hospital rather than be given a medical discharge from the service. I wanted a regular discharge so that if I had trouble making it outside the Army, I could always reenlist and return to active duty.

During our stay in North Carolina, the six of us took advantage of using a pass a few times to visit Asheville. We all would stay together, and were easy to recognize by the patches on our uniforms. Many times, people would stop to thank us for our service and ask questions about our experiences. We didn't mind, and we appreciated the interest.

Upon returning to the hospital from one trip, of all things, we happened to spot a guy who we had been imprisoned with in Japan. We were walking through the bus station when we noticed him waiting in line to purchase a ticket. We had no idea where he was coming from or where he was headed to; but the six of us immediately remembered that this guy would often say if he ever got of prison and heard the word "grourr!" (which the guards had used to summon one of us) again, he would kill the person who had said it.

We decided to have some fun. As he stood in line, we hid behind a row of seats in the station and yelled, "Grourr!" He quickly turned around, but could see no one. He must have thought he was hearing things. We then repeated the sound. This time, he jumped out of line, took out his pocketknife, opened the blade, and started on the hunt—stalking his prey.

When he came close enough to see us, he said, "Well, I'm gonna have to kill all six of you because I don't know which of you did the yelling." We all laughed and grabbed him with a big hug, and managed to settle him down. When he went back to the line at the ticket counter, he asked when the next bus would leave Asheville. The ticket agent said that in 30 minutes, two buses would be pulling out—one to New York City, and the other to Miami, Florida. He chose Miami. He really didn't care which bus he took; he was traveling the country and just wanted to get away from these ex-POW morons.

When I was released from the hospital, my orders were to report to Fort McPherson in Atlanta, Georgia, where I was to decide if I wanted to stay in the service or be discharged. Once there, I walked up to the discharge counter, and was asked by a T-5 if I was there to be discharged. I said, "Yes, sir." He asked, "On what terms?" And I answered, "On points." Servicemen were credited with a certain number of points based on where you served, how long you served, and other criteria. To get a discharge, I needed somewhere between 70 and 80 points.

He handed me a blank pad and said, "Well, Sergeant, sit over there and figure up your points." I had no idea how to do that and said, "I don't know what you get points for."

He looked a little surprised, and said, "You don't know how to figure your points? How do you know you can get out then?" At that point he looked down at the envelope holding my orders and noticed the return address of Moore General Hospital. Then he said, "Just stay there a minute." Then he walked over to the officer in charge, and I heard him say, "Captain, I think we have another nut from Moore General Hospital." (I hadn't been aware that Moore General was treating some guys with mental disorders.)

The captain said, "I'll take care of it." When the captain walked up to me, he said, "Sergeant, I understand that you wish to get a discharge, but you don't know how many points you have and don't know how to figure them."

I said, "That's right, Captain." He said, "Where have you been?" I told him I'd been overseas all during the War and spent three and a half years as a POW. He asked me, "Why didn't you tell that to the T-5?"

"Uhh…the T-5 didn't ask me that."

When the Captain figured my points, the total came to just a few less than 300. The captain then tried to get me to sign up for another three-year hitch, but all I wanted was *out*. And within a short time, I had that regular honorable discharge. I did sign up, though, for the Army Reserves.

Now I was back home with hopes of leading a normal life. The men who controlled the political strings there wanted me to run for mayor. But I wanted nothing to do with it. I didn't know for sure what I wanted to do, but I was definitely convinced that I didn't want a job where I had to do what everyone else told me to do—I had been doing that for the past four years. I wanted to enjoy the new freedom that the discharge paper gave, and I wanted to be free to do what I wanted to do for a change.

It was certainly great being home, but…there was a storm brewing inside me. It was like two different people had come home. One of them was the boy I had been before I had left in July 1941; the other was a tortured man who was still suffering inside. I was full of memories and thoughts and feelings that I could not deal with. Life was now moving so fast—much faster than I had experienced in the last four years. And I was still dealing with the fear, the suffering, the rage, and the pure hatred of the Japanese. Just several weeks ago, I was a prisoner of war in a slave labor camp on the other side of the world. Now I was supposed to adjust to a life that for four years I thought I would never live again. To my family and friends I was plain old Glenn Dowling Frazier, who happened to have served as a soldier in World War II…and now I was home again. But I knew I was no longer that person. My thoughts were often full, not of the freedom and love that surrounded me, but of the ghastly Bataan Death March, of the times that my body had been so badly beaten, and other times I was so sick that I feared I would not live another night.

Even though I was physically present with family and friends, enjoying my freedom, indulging myself with as much food as I wanted, taking a bath at least once a week, and relishing in the safety of my home, I would still wake up every couple of hours to check and see if the guy beside me had made it through the night. I could still hear the Japanese guard screaming at a fellow POW who was only trying to make his way to the slit trench to relieve himself. I could still feel the guard's rifle butt slammed against my head. I could still feel the desperate hunger and taste that soggy rice and feel the worms slide down my throat. I kept returning to the past.

I was tormented. Could I handle being back home? How would I be able to sleep without lice crawling up and down my body? Would I feel alone? Could I stand having bed sheets and blankets to cover me and keep me warm enough so that I could feel my fingers and toes? Could I stand not sleeping with a bunch of others piled up like pigs in a pen to keep warm? Would I feel awkward walking into a barbershop to get a haircut, or would I prefer again having my hair pulled out with dull scissors? Would I think it necessary to guard my food while eating? Would I feel comfortable enough to purchase my own clean undershirt or a pair of shoes? And would I want to cut holes in my shoes so my toes could stick out? Would I feel it necessary to ask permission to use the bathroom?

This had been my reality—my way of life—every moment of every day—for such a long time. And the worst part had been staring death in the face over and over, up to the point where we knew that the Jap guards had standing orders to shoot all POWs the minute an invasion took place on the mainland. Death had been my way of life. It had been my past, my present, and my future. The only comfort I had was to assure myself that the Japs would eventually get what they deserved, and that their defeat would serve as a lesson to all evil governments that when they wage war against others and treat their prisoners like animals, their despicable deeds will not go unpunished.

I was home now, and the nightmare was supposed to be over. But…it wasn't over. I wasn't adjusting from the horror or the brutality I had suffered at the hand of the enemy. In addition, I was overwhelmed with guilt and bitterness and even shame as I thought of my fallen buddies who had not been able to come home. I saw mothers, dads, sisters, and brothers waiting patiently at the pier, hoping to see their loved ones coming down the gangplank and run into their arms. Some waited for months, going back each time another ship arrived, looking just one more time. *Will he come home this time? Will I be able to recognize him? Is that him?… That's not him. Oh, I hope he comes home. I hope he comes home….*

Soon, actual nightmares started, and for many hard years they were a constant part of my life. It was easy to justify drinking my dark thoughts away and drinking until I passed out. When I had stayed at the Letterman General Hospital in San Francisco, I was told by the doctor that all I had to do was "go out and act normal." But what was I supposed to do when I couldn't act normal? When my dreams were as real to me as when I had actually been living in those horrible times? I couldn't separate my nightmares from my present life. I'd wake up feeling the lice running all over my body. I'd look for the Jap guard who was shooting the POW next to me. I'd jump and turn the lights on to see if I was still wearing the colorless Jap uniform stuffed with old cement paper to keep warm.

And I couldn't talk about these nightmares to just anyone. People would surely think I was crazy. Who could understand such an experience unless they had also survived a similar trial? Night after night, I would struggle. Each morning when I woke up, I was exhausted and felt as though I had lived the night in the prison camp. I was still battling for my own life.

I was asked the simple question time and time again, "Are you enjoying being home?" I could never say what I really wanted to.

What would people have thought had I said, "No, I'm not enjoying it. Actually, it's been hell"? I just did not know how to respond to such a question.

After being trained to fight and having to kill many times in order to save my own life and those of others around me, I accepted the fact that I was a killer—a murderer. On Bataan, I would lie in wait for a chance to slaughter a Japanese soldier. I was proud to be able to kill another of the enemy, and that became my way of life. When a day passed in which I missed an opportunity to kill another one of them, I felt like I had failed to do a good job.

Now I was back home, in a small, quiet town, where shooting a small rabbit might be the biggest news to happen in a day. I couldn't handle it. Living a normal life was unimaginable, and I became desperate. I started to think that maybe if I killed someone, it would satisfy that hidden urge within me and I would feel better. Maybe if I had been able to kill a few Japanese soldiers after my prison camp experience and before I returned home, I wouldn't be suffering so much now.

It was impossible to discuss this urge with anyone. It was an everyday fight to keep these thoughts out of my head, and I knew of no place to get help. I didn't want to go to sleep because then I would have to face the Japs again—hide…get under that bridge… run…faster…jump off that embankment…into the water…dive under that truck…get down…keep running…

The horrors of the war were with me every day and night now, and would be for the next 30 years. At times I wished I had never come home. I imagined how peaceful it would be just to lie down in a quiet place and never wake up again.

15

BUT IT WASN'T OVER

Even though I was tormented inside, the world outside was not going to pause and wait for me to fix my own problems so that I could catch up with everyone else. Life was moving ahead, and if I wanted to be a part of it, I had to move along with the rest of the world.

America had changed so much during the War...and so many people had changed as well. My relationships with family, with neighbors, with friends—all of them were different now. In fact, some of my closest friends were quite distant to me for a reason I could not fully understand. Other friends had previously moved away to work in factories to support the War effort, and women were now holding down jobs that had been held only by men before the War. Many of the women seemed to have a much more independent outlook, and I felt they weren't as friendly now. I had a lot of catching up to do.

Not long after my return, a good friend who owned a Plymouth and Dodge car dealership offered me a job. Selling cars was easy in those first days after the War. During the War, everyone had found it necessary to keep patching and re-patching their old vehicles. Now there was a waiting list of people who wanted to buy a new car, and thanks to the factory jobs that had been created during the War, they had the money to pay for them. No one was too concerned about color or style, and there was always someone ready with a handful of cash to drive away a new ride.

I was a natural salesman. Even while in high school, I had built up a good business as a Greyhound bus agent and while pumping gas. I had always maintained a strong work ethic and had been a hard worker; that part of me hadn't changed. It didn't take me long, however, to realize that selling cars was not what I wanted to do for the rest of my life. The trucking business, on the other hand, was much more interesting. America was expanding, and transporting goods across the country quickly and efficiently was necessary. While the railroads were losing business, trucks were offering door-to-door service, saving people a lot of money in handling charges.

I decided to work for a small trucking line that hauled freight between Mobile and Montgomery. I would call on businesses and increase shipments for delivery to, from, and between all the towns along Highway 31. This kind of sales offered much more opportunity, and I took advantage of my ability to "sell and close the deal."

Life was moving along well. By now I had found a girl that I wanted to marry. She said yes, and in June 1946, eight months after I had returned from the War, we were married and moved to Mobile, Alabama. But even then, I was under a lot of stress trying to adjust to any kind of normal life, and the nightmares continued. Every night I would suddenly awaken, sit up in bed, and check all around me to see if everything was okay, the same as I had done for years while in POW camps. At first, my wife empathized and expressed compassion about my fears. She tried her best to tolerate my reactions to the nightmares, as I would wake up yelling and swinging my arms, trying to defend myself against the ghosts of the past. She sincerely wanted to help me with this serious problem. But as time went on, instead of lessening their power over me, the dreams became more and more real. In fact, I felt like I had returned to Japan as a POW, and my hatred for the Japanese grew into a consuming rage.

Soon, my wife could not stand to sleep in the same room with me. She was aware of my military training and knew what kind of fighting I had been involved in while stationed in the Philippine Islands. When I reacted defensively to the nightmares, she felt her life was in danger. So we decided that I needed help from the Veterans' Administration. There, they first sent me to a psychiatrist for evaluation. In those days, meeting with a psychiatrist was like sticking a "crazy" label on me. I knew for sure that I could not tell anyone, not even my own family, that I was getting that type of treatment.

These years were difficult, and as time went on, my wife could not stand the strain of my troubles. She felt frustrated and helpless in her efforts to help me resolve them, and after six years, we entered into a separation contract in 1952 and then were later divorced.

It was hard for me to work for anyone else, so I started looking for a business that I could own—where I could be my own boss. I really enjoyed and wanted to remain with the trucking industry. It was exciting and growing, and I felt it offered me a great opportunity. So when a good friend in the moving and storage business asked me to buy a half interest in a company in Shreveport, Louisiana, I accepted and worked there as owner and manager. And because I was a veteran and a POW, I had an extra edge in acquiring transport contracts with U.S. military bases.

As I settled into the job of building my new business, I decided to take advantage of my G.I. Bill of Rights to attend college, and enrolled at the Meadows-Draughn Business College in 1947, and eventually earned a Bachelor of Science degree in business administration in 1951. While I was attending classes, the college offered a course in the Elmer Wheeler School. After taking and completing the course, I was asked to teach the course, which I did for a couple of years.

When problems with my partner in the moving and storage business began, I sold out my share and went to work with Grey Van Lines out of Chicago in 1948, becoming one of the top salesmen in the nation.

When the Korean War began, I tried to get back into the Army in 1952. However, due to my VA record of psychiatric treatment and the general state of my health at that time, I was not accepted. Then, out of the blue, Howard Van Lines of Dallas, Texas, called me and offered me the position of National Sales Manager, which required me to move to Washington, DC. I took them up on their offer and was very successful in building up the company. In a short time, we were up to 300 agents and had added 30 company offices. From 1952 to 1958, I was very busy training the entire sales force and lobbying for the moving companies in Washington.

At the end of my sixth year with Howard Van Lines, the business had grown from one million in annual sales to over 16 million. When the owners decided to cash out and sell the business, I went over to work with Greyhound Car Rental, also in Washington DC. Although I was still continuing to achieve my goals, I had a strong urge to get back into business for myself.

So in 1958, I moved to Charlotte, North Carolina, where I operated a franchise location for National Car Rental, and my business soon expanded to South Carolina. But even though my business career was moving along well, all was not well inside of me. Due to poor health, which meant that I couldn't provide personal management of the business, I found it necessary to sell out in 1963.

The same problems that I had experienced during my first marriage were now responsible for the ending of another marriage. My bitterness against the Japanese had fostered a burning and irrational hatred for them that was consuming my mind and my entire body. This black passion affected my thinking and reasoning in all areas of my life.

Eighteen years after I had returned from Japan, the severe nightmares still followed me, and I was a nervous wreck. I could barely digest my food and was exhausted. I felt as though I was strapped in—held in bondage with no say over my body or my actions. It was like being imprisoned at the camps again. I received little help from the VA because at that time, they didn't know much about the lasting effects that war and physical and mental abuse had on prisoners of war. For several years after I sold the car rental business, I drifted from job to job. I spent over a year with a Holiday Inn advertising contractor traveling all over the country. Then I went to Tampa, Florida and bought a hundred small motorcycles and rented them to riders. I sold that business and went back to Atlanta, where I started a business called Delta Car Rental. However, the partners there were very difficult to work with, so I severed my relations with them and moved to Denver, Colorado in 1967. There I became interested in tourism development, including new ski trails and lodges in the Rocky Mountains. I got involved with the Park Meadows Corporation, which built small condos in Aspen, Breckenridge, Vail, Winter Park, and Steamboat Springs.

After this experience, I decided once again to go into business on my own. I then moved to Kansas City, Missouri later that year and organized a company by the name of Glenco Development Company. I purchased 630 acres of land around the Lake of the Ozarks. I also opened an office in Denver and contracted to purchase 1500 acres between Aspen and Colorado Springs. My intentions were to build a chain of condos as vacation rentals, especially for those who enjoyed skiing. I also entered into a contract to purchase 7,800 acres west of Wheatland, Wyoming, where I planned to build a hunting lodge. I wanted to later build in Florida, close to Disney World. I envisioned a vacation exchange program for condo owners, trading for such places as the Cumberline House in Nassau, Bahamas.

Business was going quite well until the National Land Use Law was passed, and the formation of HUD made it impossible to sell your way into a development, or in other words, buy land and have it rezoned it for the building of condos and houses. In addition, it was expensive to obtain the necessary permits for building. With all of these adverse conditions, the money for development dried up.

Then, in the 1970s, we experienced the false gas shortage; consequently, it was difficult to get people interested in traveling farther than a day's drive away from their homes.

I began selling off different parcels of land. I reduced my holdings until I was down to the 630 acres on the Lake of the Ozarks, and was free and clear of debt. In 1972 I was listed in "Who's Who in the West" for my vision and work with the vacation exchange program and the progress I had made in developing the properties I owned. During a time that should have brought a feeling of great success and happiness with regard to my achievements, my life was still consumed and adversely affected due to my hatred for the Japanese.

In order to develop the 630 acres I still held, I needed a loan, which the banker promised to give me if I would agree to accept him as a partner in the deal. I concurred, and the work progressed. Then in 1977, the bank president was shot to death. The FDIC stepped in, and because my business endeavor involved the banker as a partner, I found myself in the middle of an 18-month legal battle, after which the FDIC took everything I owned—even the house I had built on the Lake of the Ozarks. The bank then reopened with new management.

In 1980 I moved to Atlanta for a year and then went on to New Orleans, where I opened a gift shop in a motel. There I met a gentleman who had a great invention—a type of engine that didn't require gasoline—and I decided to invest the money I had saved into building a prototype. I obtained a contract to manufacture and sell the product throughout the entire world. Just as the invention was ready to go into production, the inventor dropped dead of a heart attack in the late part of 1980. All the papers in his lock box proved to be worthless, and I could not find an engineer who could make it work.

During the winter of early 1981, at the age 57, I began to experience severe pain in my chest and was admitted to the Veterans'

Hospital at Iowa City with pneumonia. X-rays revealed a tumor in my right lung, resulting in surgery that cost me half of that lung.

While recovering in the Intensive Care Unit from the operation, I promised God that if He would give me one more chance, I would try my best to live a better life. Eight months later, the cancer was back. I refused chemo treatment and instead used a treatment that I obtained from members of an Indian tribe. Within 60 days, all the cancer was gone.

I then moved west again later in 1981, first to the Panhandle of Texas working with farmers trying to develop a way to pump water for their crops at a lower cost. Everything we tried failed to operate the big well pumps that we wanted to use to irrigate the large circles where they had corn, wheat, and other crops planted. I then moved farther west in 1982, this time to Arizona, where I formed a trust for the purpose of helping gold miners finance the operations of their small mines. At that time, there were no banks or even any individuals who would offer loans to gold mining operations.

After four months, I went to California in hopes of finding private investors to finance the mining. However, due to certain California laws making it troublesome to use escrow companies, I had to move on to Las Vegas, Nevada, where I could put assets into an escrow account. I made several attempts to convince investors to buy the equipment to process the ore. It was challenging trying to find trustworthy personnel to perform this process, because as soon as they saw real gold coming out of the ore, they went off on their own, leaving my operations without qualified personnel. It was a very frustrating problem, and as a result, I sold out my interest, hoping to find a less stressful business operation.

While living in the western desert area in the 1980's, my problems with the nightmares remained; and as a result, I was always in need of more rest. It became difficult to focus and maintain my energy. My anger and animosity toward the Japanese had mounted to such an extent that every time I saw an American driving one of their cars, a heated reaction would flash through my entire body. Everything in my life was being negatively affected by these destructive feelings. At times I would resort to drinking to try to forget my problems. It became impossible to tell anyone that my experiences in a war 40 years ago were still haunting me. My body was telling me that something had to be done, but I found my hatred and bitterness so strongly embedded in my heart and mind that it was impossible to do anything about it. I was reaching the end of my rope.

It was 1990 and I was 65 years old when I decided to move to Florida. At this point in my life, I had been very successful at several business endeavors, while other attempts had been a total flop. I had no idea why I prospered at times, nor could I always determine why I failed at other adventures. But I do know that God was always watching over me and had a definite plan and purpose for my life.

When I arrived in Milton, Florida, I started to attend the First Baptist Church regularly, and the church became more important to me than it had ever been. Here, people were friendlier, and I even began to meet with a Bible study group.

Early one morning, about 2 a.m., I awoke from sleep, and before I really knew what was happening, I was kneeling by my bed praying to God. It was like an uncontrollable force working inside me, even giving me the words to say. In that prayer, I asked God to help me shake the curse that was controlling me.

I had already asked my preacher at times about ways to get help and solve my problems, only to be told that I must forgive the Japanese. I said, "Oh no, I could *never* do that. They have never apologized to any of us. So, how could I do that...or why would I want to?" And I continued to suffer.

But the force within me this night as I began to pray also brought the tears. And I cried my eyes out. Every thought that passed through my mind was like a voice inside me saying, "You must forgive everyone and everything that has hurt you. You must forgive the Japanese and forgive yourself for harboring this hate for so long."

All of a sudden, I realized that the Japanese did not even know I existed, and here I was killing myself with my hatred for them. I asked God for help. In time, I learned that when each thought of resentment, or bitterness, or even a hint of a grudge would come into my mind, I would reject these thoughts and give them to God. It was a process; I had to take one day at a time, and deal with one thought at a time. And I had to pray—all the time. My life's goal was a passage from Matthew 18:21-25: *"Then Peter said, 'Lord, how often am I to forgive my brother if he goes on wronging me? As many as seven times?' Jesus replied, 'I do not say seven times; I say seventy times seven.'"*

Following this guideline was the hardest task I ever had to take on. It would take a few more years to finally cleanse my heart and body and find total release from the pain I had inflicted upon myself. I discovered that the mind, a powerful instrument, can be an enemy to the body, but it is also a marvelous gift where God's healing can begin to bring both peace and comfort to old wounds and relief from the acid bitterness that can destroy a life.

As I worked through my problems using the spiritual guidelines I had been given, I became more aware of my past feelings and the damage they had caused me. My attitude improved greatly and became more loving and tolerant of others. Before this experience in prayer, my physical health had also been failing. My diet was a disaster, so I decided to change my eating habits as well as take food supplements, such as vitamins and minerals. Making these changes was not easy, and it took almost two years to see a complete transformation in my once worn-out body and exhausted mind.

With all these positive changes came an improved physical, emotional, and mental health. And…I no longer experienced the terrible nightmares! I even visited a Honda dealership and sat in a Honda car. That was a miracle! I told my pastor that he could call the local news station and tell them that I was at the Honda dealership kissing a Honda car. The flares of hate no longer burned when I thought about the Japanese. Moreover, I was able to enter and stay in a loving relationship with a woman who continues to share my hopes and dreams.

As I studied the Word in Matthew, it became clear what had happened to me. God had changed me, and I no longer felt the bondage that had controlled me for so many years. I was free—really *free*—and able to enjoy totally new way of life.

With the help of several friends, I improved even more. I had lost a lot of time and opportunities to make a positive difference in life. But now I had the ability to live a life filled with good...filled with love...and filled with happiness.

I have learned an important lesson. The past can be remembered, but it does not have to be relived. God's peace brings the freedom within which we can accomplish our desires. Thank God, my heart is now free to love Him and *all* His other creatures. How grateful I am that I have escaped the bondage of hatred and found the freedom that forgiveness delivers.

EPILOGUE

In 1990, I returned to the Gulf Coast where I had planned to retire. While there, I visited to the National Guard to ascertain the possibility of serving in the military once again. I was directed to the Alabama State Defense Force, under the Adjutant General and part of the home front and National Guard. After reviewing my records, along with my Field Commission of First Lieutenant in the Philippine Army in 1941, they awarded me a Captain's rating. Due to years of good attendance, I was presented the rank of a Captain, then Major, then Lieutenant Colonel. After completing the required time in rank, I was promoted to the rank of Full Bird Colonel. I am still active today and plan to remain active for several more years, that is, as long as I am needed.

Now that I have personally told my life's story to family members, individuals, countless audiences and organizations, and even many times on television, I have finally been able to reconcile myself to a more normal life than the one I spent as a POW. I will never be completely released of my memories, but I have forgiven those in my past, and I am *free!*

Now, in my later years, I have chosen to use those years spent in misery and pain as a platform to help every person who will listen understand the completely helpless feeling of not being able to make even the smallest decision on your own behalf. We must preserve our country and ourselves from the danger of being controlled by others. Our freedom is a privilege every American must not take for granted. My years as a POW will not have been in vain if in doing so, others will realize how important it is to be free.

Generation Culture Transformation
Specializing in publishing for generation culture change

Visit us Online at:
www.egenco.com
www.goingebook.com

Write to: eGen Co. LLC
824 Tallow Hill Road
Chambersburg, PA 17202 USA
Phone: 717-461-3436
Email: info@egenco.com

 facebook.com/egenbooks

 twitter.com/vishaljets

 youtube.com/egenpub

 egenco.com/blog